Body Work

Body Work

stories by
Hollis Seamon

SPRING HARBOR PRESS

Printed in the United States of America

ISBN 0-935891-04-8
Library of Congress Card Number: 99-68633

Published by Spring Harbor Press in 2000
Spring Harbor Press is part of Spring Harbor, Ltd.,
Box 346, Delmar, New York, 12054
www.springharborpress.com

Cover design by Dan Dyksen.
Cover paintings by Deborah Zlotsky.
Book design by Seagull Graphics.

Spring Harbor Books may be ordered from the publisher:
Box 346, Delmar, New York, 12054.
Add a dollar for postage and handling.
New York State residents add sales tax.
Visit us online at www.springharborpress.com

This book is for my sisters,

Prilly, Libby, Rusty, and Susan,

in memory of our brother

Jim.

Acknowledgments

First, thanks to my husband, Doug Butler, and my sons, Tobias and Jacob Seamon — you guys are in these stories in more ways than you'll ever know.

Special thanks to Dan Dyksen for his generosity and skill in creating the cover design. Thanks also to Deborah Zlotsky for allowing me to use her paintings for the cover.

I would also like to thank my colleagues in the English Department at the College of Saint Rose for their unstinting generosity and support over the past ten years. Thanks, too, to the College for grants of time and money that helped in the writing of these stories. Some of the stories were written with the support of a fiction fellowship from the New York Foundation for the Arts, for which I am most grateful.

Nine of these stories have been previously published: "Learning to Bleed" in *Alkali Flats*, Fall 1999; "Gypsies in the Place of Pain" in *CALYX*, Winter 1995/96 and reprinted in *A Line of Cutting Women*, Calyx Books anthology, 1998; "Body Work" in *Chicago Review*, Volume 44, Number 2, 1998; "The Strange Sad History of Suzanne LaFleshe" in *13th Moon*, Volume XV, Numbers 1 and 2, 1997; "The Last Case of Polio in New Jersey" in *Under the Sun*, Volume 2, Summer 1997; "After the Women's Writing Retreat in Paradox, NY" in *The American Voice*, Number 39, 1996; "Sluts" in *One Meadway*, Spring 1992; "Riverkeeper" in *CPU Review*, Fall 1992; and "Middle-Aged Martha Anne" in *The Hudson Review*, Winter 1985 and reprinted in *Sacred Ground: Writings About Home*, Milkweed Editions anthology, 1996.

Contents

Body Work

Spirit Guides

N O, I'VE NEVER LEFT MY BODY," ALICE SAYS. SHE keeps her eyes down. She is balancing seven peas on her fork and feels she can't afford to look away from their precarious position on its prongs. "Never been out of it, even once. Not that I know of, anyway." She brings the peas to her mouth and sucks them in, one by one. They are olive green institutional peas, tasting more of can than vine.

The woman across the table from Alice lifts an eyebrow. "That you know of. That's my point. If you were out of your body, you might not remember, right?"

There really doesn't seem to be any answer to this, so Alice just raises her eyes and shrugs. She can't recall this woman's name. She is middle-aged, like most everyone (Alice includes herself, but just barely) at this long lunchroom table in the camp dining room. The tables are covered with variously colored and printed vinyl tablecloths and all the women are seated on thin benches pulled up to the tables, except for the very ancient women, who are given wooden chairs at the ends of tables, out of concern for their backs. The woman is a nun, of course, like everyone except Alice but it's very hard to tell: she wears huge silver earrings and her white hair is long, woven into at least twelve or thirteen braids. Nuns don't look like they used to in Alice's youth; released from habits, they all look different now. And you can't just call them all "Sister" anymore, either. They all have actual names and Alice has a good deal of name-learning to do, if she can muster the interest and energy.

The woman cuts her pork chop into little triangles and arranges them on her plate into an eight-pointed star. She then eats them quickly, one piece at a time, going counterclockwise. When the meat is all gone, she puts her fork down and looks hard at Alice. "But you had imaginary friends when you were small, didn't you?"

And just like that, they are back—the two presences (she doesn't recall them as people, really, just as, well, beings, but beings with voices, unpleasantly high-pitched voices) that three-year-old Alice knew as GoodLetter and BadLetter. One, obviously, kind; one, cruel. Alice can actually feel them here beside her, vaguely to her right, but when she looks, they are, as ever, invisible. On her right, there is only the broad denim hip of the next woman on the bench. (Alice has noticed, in just the few hours since she arrived, that nuns have bigger behinds than secular women. And they also have large, heavy breasts, oddly, since they have no use for them. Also, lovely shiny undyed hair and wide, clean faces almost free of wrinkles, testimony, Alice thinks, to lives free of makeup and men.)

"Didn't you?"

Alice looks into the soft gray eyes of the woman across

2

from her. "Yes, I did. I'd forgotten, but I did."

The woman smiles, showing a mouthful of strong crooked teeth. (Clearly, expensive orthodonture was not wasted on girls headed for the convent.) "Well, some people believe that they're not imaginary at all, those friends kids have. Some believe they're spirit visitors."

Alice feels her face go skeptical.

The woman laughs. "Really. Spirit guides, angels, whatever. Something like that." She stands, holding her tray and extracting her legs from under the table, one at a time. "I don't know," she says. "But I'm willing to believe. Well, I hope to see you at tai chi." She starts to make her way along the table to the aisle, but then she stops and adds, "Did they tell you that we've got a bodyworker coming to this retreat? One of our sisters from Chicago, a woman who's a marvelous masseuse. A miracle worker with her hands." She laughs again. "I can't wait."

Alice nods, then sits quietly sipping her tea. BadLetter and GoodLetter, spirit guides? God, she hopes not. Because, as she now recalls, she never even liked her imaginary friends much—they always poked at her, digging importunate fingers (or something) into her ribs and trying to make her (especially BadLetter, of course) do things she knew were very, very wrong.

Rootedness

The tai chi session takes place on the dock. It is a glorious fall day; the colors of the trees around the lake and on its small island are almost too bright to bear. The lake itself is deep blue and shot full of light and movement, dotted with hundreds of little whitecaps. The wind is cool and the dock moves beneath Alice's bare feet. She is trying to rock back and forth, foot to foot, exactly as the instructor demonstrates, gently and effortlessly, staying well-grounded and gracefully balanced, in tune with what the instructor calls "this beauty which surrounds us." The other women in her group are no better at this than she is and they laugh easily at themselves and one another. But they keep trying—good-natured middle-aged and old women swaying calmly in pastel sweatsuits.

Alice discovers that although she is hopeless at combining arm and foot movements, she is actually quite good at "rootedness," the essential ability, as the instructor has explained, of letting one's weight just sink into the feet and beyond, of becoming one with the ground, the earth. Even though this is in fact a splintery wooden dock which shifts with the movement of the water below it, Alice can still feel herself sinking. She is pleased with herself. She remembers that as a child and young woman, she often stood balanced on her left leg with her right foot tucked neatly behind the left knee. Her crane stance—she could hold it for hours when she was a long-legged, skinny girl. She is just beginning to feel quite competent at all of this when the instructor directs the women to cup their hands over their bellies, to find and enclose the deep well of their chi. The other women, the nuns, all do this with simple concentration, their eyes closed. But Alice's hands jump away and fall to her sides. Her belly is great with emptiness, except for the stone she carries beneath her ribs. Her breasts are rocks; she remembers, no, more than remembers, re-feels, re-experiences, the fiery pain in her breasts as the milk inside them dried and hardened, undrunk. The milk was meant for her baby girl but she hadn't lived long enough, even, to suckle. But still the milk came, then petrified in Alice's breasts. It hasn't left yet, it seems, although her doctor tells her that the hard lumps she feels there now are not milk, but just the scars from the infection all that wasted milk gave her. She stops rocking and moves off the dock. She picks up her sneakers and walks up the hill to the lodge. The pebbles on the path bruise her bare heels; she lets them.

Sister Bo Peep

Here, among the nuns, who seem honestly and simply good, Alice has already done a bad thing. She's lied on her registration form, giving a false name. She's registered as "Lisa Roberts" rather than "Alice Robbins." It's no big deal and she's not even sure why she did it, except that the name just came back to her when she was signing the slip. It was the name she'd used in college when she went to frat parties and slept with strange guys and didn't want them to track her down the next day. (As if they would bother.) Besides, in those days, "Lisa" seemed an infinitely cooler name than "Alice" and, really, it was just a variant, not quite a lie. She'd even tried, for awhile, convincing her roommate to call her "Lisa" but spelled "Li/ce." Just like the second part of her real name, of course, only with the slash so that no one could mistake it for "Lice." "Li/ce" never quite caught on, though.

But here she is again, twenty-some years later, Lisa Roberts. She's been sent here to this women's retreat, actually, by the well-meaning and concerned principal of the high school where she teaches. She's been ordered, in fact, to take her Columbus Day weekend (of course—a holiday in honor of a genocidal maniac) and to rest. Her high school is small, private—it prides itself on being a caring community which supports its members in difficult times. And it still has some old diocesan ties to this Catholic retreat site, 900 glorious acres in the Adirondacks—clean air, pristine lake, simple accommodations, wholesome food. The very goodness of the place, her principal (a former Franciscan brother himself and still wise in these matters) implied, will help her recover from the recent badness of events in her life.

Alice sits in one of the Adirondack chairs on the side deck of the old lodge. The chairs themselves are famous for their goodness—so large and sturdy and perfectly designed that you can't help relaxing in their arms, she's been told. All the chairs face the lake; she can watch the women who are using their afternoon free time to go canoeing. Other women are reading in the chairs; some are napping or meditating. The more hearty have gone hiking. Alice is just sitting, her back placed just so against the wooden support of the chair. She keeps a book in her lap, for protection, and turns a page whenever anyone glances her way and, she senses, is about to speak to her.

But she's not reading, she's resting, under orders. She puts her head back and watches leaves curling down from the maple trees. She supposes that she does need rest; just three months ago, in July, she was after all in labor, a good fifteen hours of it. And then, oh-so-briefly, in motherhood, and then in mourning. The stone of sadness that took her daughter's place under her ribs is still lodged there, solid. It is like an endless stitch in her side, as if she's been running marathons. It's there even as she sits in this perfect chair.

And, then, just last month, in September, she'd been back in school, carrying her stone and teaching English and history to sophomores and juniors, as always. There are three reasons why her principal, as he said, believes she needs this retreat: one, he thinks he understands her grief.

Two, on September 28, Alice brought a pale, stringy-haired freshman girl to tears by yelling fiercely at her in the hall, for giggling. Three, on October 8, Alice slapped the face of a football player who said he'd missed an exam because his grandfather was sick, maybe even dying. (This was an egregiously stupid lie—this kid had killed off both of his grandfathers as excuses in the past year.) Her handprint had glowed red on the boy's handsome astonished face as she had hissed at him, "Liar. You fucking little liar," right in front of her whole second period class. Then she'd slapped him again, with the other hand, just to balance the pattern on his face. More: when her principal, with sad brown eyes, told her, for the hundredth time, that he did, he truly did, understand her grief, she'd slapped him too and she had really, really enjoyed watching his eyes grow big and his hand fly shaking to his cheek. Then, horribly, he'd reached out and given her a forgiving hug as she stood, a rock, a boulder, granite in his grasp.

"Lisa?"

Alice's eyes pop open. Of course, in her one unguarded, book-free moment, someone has caught her—a tiny woman with the piping voice of a six-year-old. The woman stands next to her chair, miniature hands folded neatly across her tummy. She is wearing a pale green pantsuit and white Keds; there is a purple fanny pack around her waist.

"Yes?" Alice says. She knows this woman's name, sort of. She's already heard some of the other nuns calling her, when she can't hear them, "Sister Bo Peep." Not her real name, of course, but uncannily apt.

"I just thought I'd introduce myself," the woman says. She sits down in the chair beside Alice's and scoots her tiny hips (an exception to the broad-butt rule) back against the chair and straightens her legs in front of her. Her feet stick straight out, so far from reaching the ground that Alice has to turn her face away. It seems rude to stare, but who could help it? This is the smallest grown woman Alice has ever seen.

Sister Bo Peep smiles shyly. "I'm Sister Mary Alice," she says. "I'm seventy-five years old."

Alice jumps at hearing this other variant of her own real name and now she does stare. There is not a line on this woman's face. "Really?" she says.

"Oh yes." She closes her eyes and raises her face to the breeze. The sun makes a halo of her short white hair.

Alice stares harder. "You look much younger. What do you do?" She doesn't know if this is an appropriate question—maybe seventy-five-year-old nuns don't have to do anything, really.

But Sister Mary Alice smiles. "Not very much, anymore. I help take care of the elderly sisters in the Mother House." She opens her eyes. Either they're reflecting the flawless sky or they really are the purest blue Alice has ever seen. "I taught kindergarten for fifty years or so, before that."

Of course, Alice thinks. Only kindergartners would be smaller than this woman and still innocent enough not spend their days planning ways to torment her. Alice is sure that Sister Mary Alice never, even once, slapped one of her students. She can't think of a thing to say, except what pops out: "The Mother Ship?" She knows that's wrong as soon as she hears it but Mary Alice smiles.

"The Mother House, dear. Where I live now." She giggles. "I think the Mother Ship is on *Star Trek*. Where they all fly back to in the end, isn't it?" She nods and closes her eyes again. "That's what I think."

"Oh." Alice intends to say nothing, nothing else at all, but her mouth springs open again and she says, "Are you a virgin?"

Mary Alice's eyes stay firmly shut but she answers calmly,

as if she's been asked this question every day of her life. "Oh yes." She sighs a little and crosses her tiny ankles. They hover at least ten inches off the ground. "I said I would be, you know, and so I am."

Alice's eyes feel as if they will fill with tears but the stone in her side, as always, absorbs the moisture before it flows. "I am, too," she says. This silly lie comes out of her mouth in a voice which is definitely not her own—that shrill BadLetter (or GoodLetter—they sound exactly the same) voice which Alice remembers from her childhood. "I had a baby but I'm still a virgin."

Mary Alice nods, eyes still closed. "Well. That's happened before, hasn't it?"

Alice sits up straight, pushing her throbbing side hard against the arm of her perfect chair. She leans toward Sister Mary Alice. "My baby died," she whispers. The words seem to float out of her mouth and rise up in the breeze. She's not sure if they are even audible.

But they must be, because Mary Alice answers. "Oh yes, I know," she says. Her eyes open and she looks up at Alice's face above her own. "Father Bernard told us why you were joining our retreat. He told us not to mention babies." She laughs and raises one tiny hand and lays it, light as a leaf, on Alice's arm. "Isn't that like a man? To think you'd forget if we never said 'baby.'" She leans back and shuts her eyes again. "The Mother House," she says, "is called Our Lady of Perpetual Sorrows. I have my own room there, with a lovely blue rug and flowers on my bedspread."

Bodyworker

At four p.m., the women gather in the lodge living room

to meet the nun who is a bodyworker. They sit in a loose circle of musty wicker and wooden chairs, as the bodyworker speaks. She is quite young, for a nun. (So few are young, Alice has noticed. Who will take care of Sister Mary Alice, she worries, when even she admits to being elderly? Why are there so many wise mothers and so few daughters?) She is a small sturdy woman in a bright cotton dress that falls to her ankles. She wears sandals over bare feet. Her name is Beth, she says, and she explains that she is a licensed massage therapist, that she offers half and full hour sessions, that she will focus on any one trouble spot or the whole body. She is here, she says, to help all of these women relax and enjoy their corporeal selves. They all work very hard, she knows, at their jobs and here on retreat they deserve a bit of pampering. She will begin this afternoon and continue through the weekend, working in the old boathouse.

One nun, a woman who Alice has already noticed is often loud and who, she's heard, is a former biker chick with tattoos on her ass, and who teaches math to seventh graders in some horrible inner city school, yells out from the back of the room: "Listen, ladies. I've had one of Beth's massages. Believe you me, she'll make you feel so damn good that you may have to marry her, afterward."

Some of the nuns laugh; others shake their heads. But they all line up to sign Beth's sheet. Alice tries to walk out of the room quietly, with no intention of signing up for bodywork, ever, but before she crosses the threshold her arm is caught and she is looking into the dark eyes of the rowdy biker nun, who is grinning. "Hey, Lisa," she says, "you're first. We put you down for the first time slot, kiddo."

Alice tries to pull her arm away but this woman is strong—her forearms are circled by a design of twisting blue snakes. "Thank you," Alice says, "but I...."

"But shit," the woman says. "We already paid, so you're going. Your appointment is in ten minutes."

The boathouse is dusty and cool. It has small windows set high in its plank walls and specks drift in the light that comes slanting down from above. It smells of old varnish and canvas. In the center, Beth has set up a table, padded with quilts and surrounded by screens made of Indian print bedspreads. There is a whole line of candles waiting to be lit and an array of aromatic oils set out on a bench.

The first thing Alice does is sneeze. She stands just inside the door and says, "I appreciate this, but I don't want a massage."

Beth looks up from where she is arranging a pile of clean white towels. She nods. "Okay."

So simple: Alice doesn't quite know what to do. She begins to back up through the open doorway.

"But the sisters paid for a half hour for you. So maybe you can just stay and talk, so their feelings won't be hurt. Or you can help me set up."

Alice shakes her head. "I'm sorry, I can't. I think I'm allergic to those oils or something." As if to prove it, she sneezes again.

Beth smiles. "Okay. So we'll go to the loft." She points to a ladder and a wooden platform above it.

Alice really doesn't want to hurt anyone's feelings. She climbs the ladder behind Beth, watching her strong brown calves on each step above her. Her own legs, pale and skinny, are wobbly on the rungs.

The loft is small, lit by a two-paned window so grimy there is no view. But there is plenty of light, a pale wash of light over everything. Beth and Alice sit side by side on the floor, leaning back against the rough wooden planks of the wall. "So why don't you want a massage, Lisa?" Beth asks. She settles her long skirt around her knees; the pattern on the cotton is orange and green, jungly.

Alice leans her head back. She can feel cobwebs and sawdust getting in her hair. "I'm too sore," she says. "It will hurt."

Beth is drawing little designs in the dust on the floor. "I don't hurt people," she says.

Alice nods. "I'm sure you don't try to but, believe me, it hurts."

Beth doesn't answer. She is humming a little and creating a series of clumsily-drawn daisies along one floorboard. They look like the work of a rather slow four-year-old.

Alice looks at the daisies and laughs. The stone in her side shifts and she puts a hand over her ribs.

Beth looks up. She blows a wad of dust off her index finger and points toward Alice's middle. "That where it hurts most?" she says.

Alice shrugs. "There. And here." She puts her palms over her breasts. She can feel how rigid they are, how ungiving. The high voice comes back and says, for her, "My baby was missing all kinds of organs. She was perfect, outside, but they said she had no real brain and no real kidneys and probably lots of other things." She crosses her arms over her chest and lowers her head to her bent knees. "I've thought and thought and I think I've figured out why. Why she was so...so incomplete."

Beth nods. "Uh huh. So, why?"

"I think maybe it was because I got her from a guy I didn't love. Hell, I didn't even like him much. I just took his sperm. I didn't call him, after I knew I was pregnant. It was simple: I was forty and I wanted a baby. But nothing else. No love, no friendship, no marriage, nothing. Nothing from him but his sperm, easy as pie. I doubt if he re-

12

members my name."

Alice feels Beth shift on the floor beside her. She can't turn off the shrill voice coming from her mouth. "So she was just kind of empty, my little girl. I held her—she was warm and pink and chubby. Beautiful, but light as air. She lived nineteen hours. The nurses gave me a small room with a rocking chair and I held my baby for nineteen hours. I didn't even get tired. She was very light." Alice's neck hurts but she can't lift her head. "But now," she says, "she's gotten really heavy."

Beth lays a dusty hand on the back of Alice's neck. "Lisa, I'm so sorry," she says.

Alice feels the warmth of that hand, its specific gravity and its kindness. It's the kindness, the terrible sympathy, that burns, acid on her skin. She jerks her head up and tosses off the hand. "Don't touch me," she says, in her own voice. "I can't stand to be touched." She scrambles to her feet. She is dizzy and shaking. "And my name is Alice, not Lisa. How come no one can remember my fucking name?" She goes down the ladder as fast as she can, backwards, on trembling legs.

Beth's face appears in the opening above the ladder. Her head is fuzzy with light. "If you loved her," she says, "she was not empty."

Forked

The last thing Alice wants is supper but she is sure that if she doesn't show up, some infinitely kind sister with the face of an angel will bring a tray to her room. She's had it with this whole thing, but the cool part of her mind knows that her job probably depends on her staying, on her at least pretending that she is actually trying to, as her principal says, move beyond this. "You certainly can't go on abusing your students," he'd said. "Parents are already complaining. They spend a good deal of money to send their children here; they will not put up with this."

So she sits in the dining hall and tries to eat small bites of beef stew. But the stone has grown even larger since this afternoon and now it is enormous in her belly and chest, reaching up into her throat. She has trouble swallowing and can only manage tiny sips of gravy.

The talk and laughter of the nuns sweep around her. Before the meal, they gathered and sang, "Bless our friends, Bless our food, Bless our time here together," to the tune of "Edelweiss." She'd had to quell a BadLetter mockery of such stupid, simplistic goodness and keep her eyes on the floor until the song ended. Now she keeps her eyes on her tray; no one even tries to speak to her.

Halfway through the meal, there is a commotion at one of the other tables. A chair is thrown over and people begin shouting. Alice looks over. Sister Mary Alice is lying on the floor in the aisle between tables. She is perfectly calm and quiet, her hands folded on her chest. Her mouth is open, like a baby bird waiting for its dinner. Sisters are buzzing around her, whispering "Heimlich" and "ambulance" and "stroke." But then Beth steps over Mary Alice's body and, bending over her, pulls a fork out of the patient open mouth. Beth holds up the fork for everyone to see— one of its prongs is cruelly bent and the fork, apparently, had caught in the roof of Mary Alice's small mouth. It has done absolutely no damage, however, probably because Mary Alice remained so placid. She did not fight it, did not even bite down. She simply laid herself down on the floor and awaited deliverance. She is, though, just a bit shaken and two of her sisters help her back to her room.

The minute she is gone, the nuns erupt into loud laughter. They bend their faces into their hands, giggling wildly and wiping tears from their red cheeks. A prayer, started by the biker nun, runs up and down the tables: "Dear Mother of God," it goes, "let us learn from this event. Let us never forget the night that the Virgin Mary Alice got forked and how she just laid back and enjoyed it."

It's funny and their laughter is contagious. Alice smiles but she cannot force joy from her swollen throat.

Sirens

At eight-thirty that night, most of the sisters are in the boathouse, line dancing. Even the oldest of the women are stamping and clapping from their chairs on the sidelines and the music sweeps out the open door into the darkness.

Alice pled fatigue and went to her room right after supper. No one tried to stop her although a round woman with springy gray curls asked if she could bring her some ice cream, later. "We always have sundaes," she said, "after we dance, when we're on retreat. It's a great treat."

Again, a shrill voice in Alice's head sniggered and whispered, "Who are these people, with their fucking Edelweiss and their ice cream? Why don't they just grow up?" But she had said, simply, "No. No, thank you, sister. I'll be fine."

But of course she isn't fine; the weight in her chest is so heavy that she has come out into the cold night air to catch her breath. She sits crosslegged on the dock, trying to expand her lungs. She hasn't taken a deep breath in three months, it occurs to her, and she's pretty sure that now her lungs are actually failing, that they've given up, gone all sticky and gelatinous. Every day they admit less and less oxygen.

She is very still here in the dark and so the three sisters

who have snuck off from the line dancing to take a night-time canoe ride don't even see her. Taking a canoe out after dark is strictly forbidden; Alice has seen the sign that says so. But these three are not worried. They are excited, she can hear it in their giggling and whispered cursing as they clamor into a canoe. Alice doesn't recognize them in the darkness of the cove by the dock but as the canoe glides out into the black waters there is enough light from a sliver of moon for her to discern the biker nun sitting in the stern, her strong arms working the paddles. In the bow, she thinks, is Beth. The third woman, wrapped in a dark hooded sweatshirt, she cannot place. She could be any one of them.

The canoe rides a narrow streak of silver light for a few minutes and then it moves into the shadow of the island and then it is, simply, invisible. Alice strains her eyes, shivering, wrapping her arms around her chest, but the canoe has disappeared. Behind her, the music of the line dancing stops and she hears the women pour out of the boathouse, laughing and talking. They form a stream of sound as they make for the dining hall and their sundaes. When the dining hall door slams behind the last of them, a terrible lonely silence falls. It coats Alice and the lake.

She bends forward, her hands on her ankles, pulling herself into a tight ball. The pain in her chest and in her side and in her empty belly is, suddenly, far more than she can bear. It really is, a voice says in her ear, just too much. And it will never ever stop.

Alice rocks back on her haunches. From the lake, far out, there is a sound. She can't place it at first, but then it comes clear. It is singing. Three-part harmony in sweet high voices. Alice lifts her head, freeing an ear. The three voices wind and blend in an old song. Alice doesn't know its name. Maybe it has no name—it's just an old lullaby, a simple, anonymous cradle song. Somewhere, out in the black waters, the nuns are singing to the babies they will never bear.

Alice stands and lifts her arms above her head. She balances easily on one leg and dives. The water is icy and closes around her like iron but she lifts her head and swims, going toward the voices.

The Body Left Behind

On the cold dark dock, three women bend frantically over the still body of a fourth. They are stripping off her soaked clothes, rubbing her hands, her feet. She seems not to be breathing. She seems very peaceful. But cold, terribly cold.

Beth gives orders. "Take off your clothes," she tells the other two, and they do, stripping right down to their skins, blue in the moonlight. "Now lie down with her," Beth says. "Hold her. Warm her up."

They do that, too, lying right down on the hard dock and taking the icy flesh of the drowned woman into their strong arms. Beth throws all of their shed clothes over them and then she kneels down. She takes the dripping head into her hands, bending it back to clear the throat. The woman gags and begins to shake. The sisters hold her as tightly as they can. One begins to croon to her, softly.

"Alice, Alice?" Beth says. She holds the wet head between her trembling knees. She gives one cheek a sharp slap. "Alice," she says, "come on. Breathe. Breathe."

Alice finds herself, heated and compressed between walls of strong flesh which cling to her on all sides. Her head is being pulled forward. She is being pressed, squeezed. She hears wordless sounds of comfort and then her name being called. There is a great pressure in her belly and the stone shatters. She gasps and her lungs expand. Her throat opens and she wails. She wails and wails and wails and the three women wail with her, their voices mounting to the quiet sky.

The Strange Sad History of
Suzanne LaFleshe

LISTEN, EVERY DAY YOU ARE BEING TAUGHT to hate and fear your own flesh. You are told that good food—food sweet and rich and whole—will kill you; you are told that good sex—sex rich and whole and sweet—will kill you. You can hardly imagine, anymore, what it is to love your flesh for the pleasures it provides, to honor even fat as bounty and to find joy in plenitude.

Here is a story for you. It may not be strictly true, nor exactly instructive, but it is a real story, and I offer it to you. It didn't come out as I'd planned and I'm not sure yet how it ends but for now, this is it: the strange sad history of me, Suzanne LaFleshe.

This story began last summer. By mid-July, I was fat again. Not fat enough, but growing. I could feel the old familiar flesh gathering about my ribs and thighs; my breasts were already straining against the new lace C-cup bra I had bought for them just a few months before. My table glistened with cream and eggs and sugar. I was getting rich, again.

Janet, the woman who had been weighing me in regularly at Weight Watchers, didn't say anything, the first week that the scale went up three pounds. She just smiled and shook her head a bit. The next week—another five pounds up—she looked a little alarmed. "Suzanne," she said, bowing her head over my chart and avoiding my smiling eyes, "is something wrong? I mean, we all backslide at times, after reaching our goals, but we don't usually slide back so fast, if you know what I mean." She raised her eyes when I laughed.

"Yeah," I said. "I'm sliding along here like a fiberglass toboggan—whoosh." I drew a steep descent in the air with my hand, pleased at feeling the beginnings of the old jiggle in my upper arm. "Sliding back like a son-of-a-bitch."

Janet stepped back, away from the scale, and looked at my arm. I could actually see the distaste growing on her face. She ran her bony hands down her size-5 navy linen skirt and retucked her sleeveless lemon yellow blouse: not a quiver on those tan arms. Once, she had told me, she had weighed 203 pounds; now she held steady at 97. A true transfiguration: I admired her for it. It just wasn't the kind I wanted; I'd learned that it wasn't what I wanted, the way we learn most things in life, after I'd gotten it.

Please understand: I like my flesh. I like the way it moves and bounces; I like to see my breasts floating high, like islands in the bath; I like the sensation of my thighs squeezing together in stockings, caressing each other under one of my favorite full flowered skirts. I like introducing myself, to strange men in bars, as Suzanne LaFleshe and seeing if they smile. (If they're too drunk or too stupid to get it, I know I can forget about them, move on, find

20

another.) I like to see the little-boy-lost looks on their faces when they lean over and see, for the first time, the actual scope of my breasts under my white cotton peasant blouse, the kind with the puffy sleeves and deep scoop neck. I like to see that gratitude, the absolute relaxation, the flash of joy when they realize that here, here, is a place they could die, happy.

But I felt a little sorry for Janet. She really had been pleased about my progress, all last winter and spring. She'd sent me a congratulations card for every 10-pound loss. She'd sent flowers when I'd lost 100 and she'd thrown a little party—diet soda and ice milk and sugar-free cookies—at the Weight Watchers center when I'd reached my goal: 145 pounds. (Hey, I'm tall, 5'11", so 145 really was thin, believe me. Hell, I'd started at 282. And that's where I was heading again, sliding as fast as I could, on runners greased by butter.) So I took her hand, trying not to be scared by its frailty, her bones so hard in my soft palm. Her head barely reached my shoulder.

"Listen, Janet," I said, leading her to a chair in the corner of the room, away from the chattering groups of women lining up for the scale. "Sit down."

She sat, pulling her skirt over her tiny brown knees. Her legs were so small they made me want to weep.

"Listen, it's not your fault. I just want to be fat again. I miss it." I sat down and crossed my legs, listening for that sweet sigh as they slid together. My summer sandal, size 11, special order, showed my toenails, newly painted, a nice clear shade of plum. (Listen, I keep myself clean, polished, shaved, deodorized, shampooed like everyone else. I'm not some evil-smelling fat woman. Oh, I smell: I smell like your grandmother's kitchen, touched by cinnamon and nutmeg, by yeast and warm bread-dough, rising. I smell like your mother's breasts, before you can really remember them: milky, warm, and solid.) I patted her knee.

Janet folded her hands in her lap, a patient teacher. "Oh, come now, Suzanne," she said. "You're just experiencing a perfectly normal letdown. There's always a little of that after you've reached your goal. A kind of anticlimax, after you've really done it. You know, like the day after Christmas." Janet's eyes, light blue in her tanned face, looked at me with absolute expectation of agreement.

I could see the wrinkles gathering at the corners of her eyes; skin without any fat behind it has nothing to do but fold in on itself—it's inevitable. My face had collapsed, too, but it was reviving. I could feel the fat cells bolstering up my cheeks; like pillows when they're shaken, my cheeks were plumping up nicely. I was always lucky about my face anyway. I had never been one of those fat women who lose their eyes among the rolls and who always look squinty. No, my face just rounded to a certain point and then stopped, full but not piggy. I retained a neck, I acquired no extra chins. I always carried my weight, fortunately, between my shoulders and knees. My ankles stayed trim enough, always, to wear a thin gold anklet: you know, the kind your mother told you were cheap and vulgar and sluttish? Yes, one of those. And your mother was partly right—anklets are sluttish in that men do love them and they do seem to hope for extraordinary sexual adventures with women who wear them. But, then, men hope for the same from women who wear hair ribbons and other small adornments, too. I think that men are just always hopeful and they are, so often, let down. I hate to disappoint them, ever. One spring, years and years back, in my college English-major-cum-hippie days when I was a gloriously fat young woman, I even wore a small circlet of silver bells around my left ankle, like a Morris dancer ringing in Spring. The bells jingled, very slightly, whenever I moved my leg. In stuffy college classrooms, those bells brought April in and brought college boys to my dorm room, night after night: boys young and fresh and unthinkingly cruel as April itself. And a few professors came to call, too, bringing their Prufrock poetry and middle-aged sadness. Who could bear to turn them away?

Anyway, I had always kept my youthful ankles and I was one of those fat women that you see on dance floors everywhere, having more fun than anyone else, spinning on slim high heels, moving with the impossible, gravity-defying grace of tops and dreidels. So light on her feet, people say, it's amazing. Grace is always amazing, isn't it? No less so to those of us who have it, believe me.

"No," I said to Janet. "It's not that kind of letdown." I looked at my toes; their painted roundness pleased me. "I lost the weight, I guess, because I was curious to see if I really could. But it didn't make me happy, not at all. I guess I just like being fat, better."

"Nonsense." Janet almost snorted out the word. I was glad she could make such a rude noise; it meant there was hope for her, too. "Nonsense," she repeated, more calmly. "No one likes being fat. That's just a common psychological defense mechanism."

I shook my head. What could I say, to convince a woman who could take pop psychobabble seriously? I tried: "Janet," I said, "listen. I miss myself—I miss the all-of-me I've always been." She wasn't listening, I could tell; she was preparing her next salvo of common sense. I stared into her dark, frail, wrinkled face. "Listen, Janet," I said. "I miss all the men. Men like to fuck fat women. No: they love to fuck fat women. Remember?"

She went pale, under the surface, and she stood up. "I didn't hear that, Suzanne," she said, lips tight, jaw tight. "I did not hear that." She walked away, navy pumps clicking quickly over the tiled floor. Ass tight.

But I knew that she had heard me and I know that she missed it too, the richness of full-fleshed sex. Janet remembers this, but how can I possibly explain it to you, who haven't known it? I'll try. Listen, it is my own flesh I most love when making love. My flesh moves, wave after wave, all around me. I—the me who lives inside this flesh, feeling—I am like the core, the slim tight core at the center of a storm of sex. The man—and I like tough, thin men although I'm not really picky—the man is the catalyst; he provides the straight hard axis on which I turn. If he's good—and most men are good, really they are—then he joins me, somehow, on the inside of the whirlwind. Together, we set the flesh in motion, with our primitive bumps and grinds and shivering sliding thrusts and pulls, but once begun, it moves us. From my thighs to my breasts, the waves heave and peak, heave and peak. The man is lost; I am lost. He comes once; I lose count.

I'm not saying this quite right, am I? I'm not really capturing it and it sounds like one of the steamier Harlequin romances. Plainly then: pound for pound, my fat multiplies my orgasms. It's really that simple.

Anyway, that day, I left Weight Watchers and went home for lunch. I made a loaf pan of rice pudding, my grandmother's recipe, full of real cream and covered with a rum-laced hard sauce, and ate it all, slowly, rolling each grain of warm plump rice on my tongue. Nothing nourishes like rice pudding.

For the next few weeks, Janet weighed me silently. She noted the growing pounds—6 one week, 8 the next, 9 the next—on my chart, with no comment. But then I guess she broke under the pressure of my mounting flesh and when I went in on a hot August Tuesday, on my lunch hour as always, she met me with a small Weight Watchers delegation. They introduced themselves not by name but by position: one thin woman, the regional manager; and one comfortingly chunky man, the local representative. Janet took us all to a tiny office. I sat in one of the four wooden chairs and deliberately spread myself out. My legs took up most of the floor space and they all had to sit with their feet tucked up under their chairs. They looked very uncomfortable and I relaxed.

The regional manager spoke first. "Well, Suzanne. Or do you prefer Ms. Brown?"

"Suzanne," I said. "Suzanne LaFleshe."

Three faces went blank, then the local rep chuckled. He'd gotten it. I put him down, mentally, as a possibility. I'd already checked his wedding band finger and it was empty, except for the ghost of an old indentation of, maybe, ten years of marriage, awhile back. Definitely a possibility. The regional manager stared him down. "A joke," I said, sweetly. "That's just my fat name. You know, like writers have pen names and actors have stage names? I have a fat name."

No one even smiled, although the local rep looked like he wanted to.

"Ms. Brown will do," I said.

She nodded. "Well, Ms. Brown. Janet tells us that you're upsetting the other clients. That you are deliberately gaining weight, that you undermine her every effort. You bring," she glanced down at a report, typed up, I supposed, by Janet and sent out in triplicate. "You bring recipes to the other women, recipes full of fat and sugar." She shuddered.

The local rep coughed softly into his copy of the report. I really did like him. "Only one recipe," I said. "My grandmother's ice box cake, filled with chocolate custard and iced with whipped cream. I brought it in for Bonnie's little girl's birthday, that's all. She wanted something special, so I..."

She held up a slim hand, palm outward, to stop me. "The point is, Ms. Brown, we would like you to stop coming to Weight Watchers," she said. "You are making mock of us."

I appreciated her wording—"making mock" sounds good—but I said, "I've already paid for the next six months. I want to come; I want to keep track of my gain. I want to follow it, see it grow. I want to watch my weight. Isn't that what you people want us to do at Weight Watchers?"

She stared. "We will refund your money," she said.

"No, thank you." I stood up, tall and large and strong. "I prefer to keep coming in." I went to the door, then turned to face them. "I won't bring anymore recipes, though," I said nicely, in order to make a graceful exit. My grandmother, a fine large woman who died in her garden at the age of 97, unslimmed by time or sorrow, taught me that: "Suzanne," she'd say, "always leave a room well. Make them remember you."

And I know for sure that the local rep, whose name turned out to be Chuck, remembered, because he took my home number off my chart and called me that same evening. We spent three nights in a row in my oversized bed, reviving his memories and his spirit (and mine) and his love for his body (and mine), and then I sent him on his way, happy. I don't like to keep men for more than three or four nights, generally; life is too short to waste on repetition. And Chuck, of course, as a Weight Watchers representative, couldn't really afford to take me anywhere or be seen in public with me: me, the embodiment of all that Weight Watchers loathes and profits from. Actually, few men are that brave and I don't expect it. Men are very fragile human beings and it is for that, really, that I love them.

Anyway, after that Tuesday I went in quietly, once a week, and Janet weighed me, quietly, and I felt myself growing richer and richer, in peace. I was up to 200 and still gaining when Janet pulled her rabbit from a hat and defeated me. I admire that woman, really I do. She is far more devious than I'd imagined; many skinny women are. Maybe that's all they have left of their former fat selves— guile. But I think that they too, like you, have been beguiled, charmed into being the serpents in their own gardens.

Because when I went into Weight Watchers one cool September Tuesday at 12:30 as usual, there was a new girl on the scale right in front of me. A girl maybe fourteen or fifteen. A skeletal girl, shivering in a tank top and shorts: arms like matchsticks, legs like a stork. Hair dyed that awful flat black the kids use and sheared off on one side. Skin like the bottom of a dry creek bed, gray and cracked and hopeless. The scale read 83 pounds; I was close enough to read it before she stepped off and pulled on a black sweatshirt, sizes and sizes too big. She walked away and sat down by the long wall mirror, her head bent against her pulled-up knees.

Janet looked at me, triumph shining in her pale eyes. She smiled. "Suzanne," she said, "how are you? Lovely skirt. Hop on the scale, please."

I was suspicious of all the pleasantness but not enough to leave, to just haul myself out into the sunshine and let it go. It took her a long time to adjust the weights on the scale, they'd been moved so far down for that girl.

She fiddled with the weights for a while and then said

cheerily, "206," and marked my chart.

I stepped off, smoothing my skirt against my thighs. She put her hand on my arm. I could feel the determination in her fingers. She hated touching me. She was afraid of my flesh. Afraid that her tight bony little hand would be pulled in, somehow, absorbed and lost. Seduced by Suzanne LaFleshe. But she was tough—she held on, her pink nails making little red crescents in my forearm.

"Perhaps you would like to meet Theresa, our new client?" she said. She leaned closer, standing on her toes, straining to reach my ear, and whispered, "Theresa is a problem case, poor thing, recommended by Social Services. She thinks she's fat, imagine. Anorexia, of course." She released my arm and I looked at the four moons her nails had left in my flesh. Then she spoke in a normal tone, sure of my attention. "They're hoping we can change her view of food, teach her the benefits of healthy food habits. Perhaps you can help her, Suzanne."

There was still time to leave but I couldn't. I was already walking toward Theresa.

"And, Suzanne," Janet said to my back, "Theresa's been sexually abused, so please be careful what you say to her, okay?"

I turned to see Janet's eyes fixed on my feet, on my cheap and vulgar and sluttish and lovely anklet. "Abused?" I said.

Janet nodded. "By her own father, apparently. Repeatedly. Since she was four or five, the social worker said."

For one moment, I had to picture that: a tiny little girl pinned beneath her heavy father. The sexual proportions all wrong, all backwards: no flesh to protect her. No joy. I felt ill.

Janet smiled. "There are lots of ways to destroy yourself, Suzanne," she said. "You choose to eat; she chooses not to. Go say hello."

Theresa didn't look up at first, while I struggled to put myself on the floor beside her. It wasn't easy for me to get onto a floor but I did it, landing finally in a position where I could lean back on the mirror and stretch my legs out straight. But by the time I'd settled, Theresa was staring, running her eyes over the expanse of my body.

"Hi," I said, holding out my hand. "I'm Suzanne. Suzanne LaFleshe."

For a second she just looked blankly polite, then she giggled. She put her hand, dry and thin as a fallen leaf, in mine. "Hi," she said. "I'm T-bone."

I laughed. "You certainly are," I said.

That night, I went to a new bar. I liked to change my bars frequently so that I didn't become a regular—the resident loose and easy fatso. I perfumed and shaved and lotioned and shampooed and dressed up carefully, as if for a special occasion. I picked a bar with country/western on the jukebox. They're the simplest, really, with the nicest guys: unpretentious, up-at-5, work-till-5, dance-till-midnight, fuck-till-dawn guys. To me, it didn't much matter if they read books, or wrote them: what I wanted was a poet of the flesh. Lots of men are, more than you'd think from reading Cosmo questionnaires and from listening to thin women gripe. Trust me, lots of men are.

Listen, when you're fat, you learn early how to find nice guys. I learned a lot in high school: the boys in my advanced-level college prep classes wouldn't give me a glance, or if they did, it was just to entertain their friends with fat-girl jokes. (Here's a sample. Question: How do you figure out where to fuck a fat girl? Answer: Roll her in flour and aim for the wet spot. I didn't make this up: who could? Think about that: who could?) So I got a D in fancy-ass advanced algebra my freshman year and, the next year, got placed in dumb-ass plane geometry, the only girl in a class of 25 greaser hoods. It was heaven; those guys were wonderful. I learned a lot about sex and cars, simultaneously. I taught some of them to love geometry, its precise angles and its generous truths; they taught me appreciation of my very own physical universe: more than fair bargain. And my geometry teacher, a brusque Korean war vet, took me aside once and said, "I looked up your IQ, Suzanne. It's very high. Did you know that? Did anyone ever tell you exactly how high it is?" "No," I said. "And please don't, okay?" And he, probably because he too was a nice guy and a survivor of a complex life, didn't.

High school geometry served me well my whole life. I could shoot pool with experts, dancing around the table on slim high heels, flashing my anklet, letting my breasts hang over the cue. I moved the cue up and down, deliberately, between my breasts, up and down, then aimed and shot. I'd have a man ready for my bed before the game was half over. It was almost too easy.

Anyway, I chose carefully the night following my lunch with Theresa. His name was Dexter; imagine life as a Dexter. But he hadn't shortened it or resorted to nicknames; I admired that. He was around 45, graying and shy, and he needed the solace of the flesh as much as I did. He chose, from my assortment of condoms—yes, I too had given in to this one form of necessary caution, even though I sorely missed the sensation of skin on skin—my favorite, the deep deep blue. It's funny how that color can make a penis look dangerous, interesting, even a little mysterious, when essentially, as you and I both know, it is not. Dexter stayed until 6 a.m., when he had to go to work. He asked if he could come back for supper. He asked if I'd like to go out dancing. Here was a man not afraid to be seen with me—a find. But I said, no. No thanks, to both suggestions. I said goodbye. As I say, it was an occasion.

That day I met Theresa in the park for lunch. I'd brought a lot of food, but it was really just my usual lunch. Theresa sat on the grass, her Q-tip legs folded in front of her. Her eyes got bigger and bigger as I spread out the food on the blue-checked cloth: six pieces of fried chicken, a bowl of potato salad, half a loaf of zucchini bread, and two slices of chocolate pound cake, my grandmother's recipe. I poured milk from my thermos: unskimmed, high fat, real milk.

I leaned back against a tree. September was all around us, rich with smells. I put a napkin on my lap and began to eat. Theresa sat still at my side. I offered her some of everything I ate, chicken, salad, bread, and cake, but she just shook her head. "No, thanks," she said. "I'm not hungry. I had a big breakfast."

I nodded. "That's good. As Janet always says, 'Eat breakfast like a king, lunch like a prince, and supper like a pauper.' Right?" I grinned. I do a pretty fair Janet imitation, even now: lips pursed, throat tense, everything tight.

Theresa giggled. She put a blade of grass between her lips and sucked on it. She looked like an Irish famine victim; I'd read once how they had died with their lips dyed green from eating grass, the only harvest their tired land would produce. Her cheeks were intensely pale and hollow, her eyes a strange dull brown. Her shaved skull glowed through its fringe of dark hair: a black and white girl, all edges, no compromise. My chest actually hurt when I looked at her, as if one of my chicken bones had gone down sideways and lodged there. I felt the dangers of living inside that body, its bones so clear, no padding for any kind of fall.

I didn't press food on her; I just ate it in front of her, sucking on bones, licking chocolate crumbs from my fingers, one by one. Her eyes never strayed from the food. "Janet says," I said, when I was done, every scrap gone. "Janet says you think you're fat. Do you?"

Theresa rolled her eyes. "Janet's a jerk," she said. The piece of grass fell out of her lips and she replaced it with a stick.

"Yeah, well, that is certainly true." I leaned back on the tree with a sigh and let myself spread out over the grass. I folded my hands on my belly and looked down over the field of my flesh. "Now, me. I'm fat," I said. "That's obvious."

She laughed. "Yeah."

I nodded. "So, if I'm fat, what are you?"

She stretched herself out next to me, imitating my position exactly. "I," she said, "am not fat. I am a twig. You're a whole tree."

I laughed: the kid had class.

She looked up into the leaves, just beginning to turn color. "I am T-bone, the twig. I have an official eating disorder, you know." She laughed and I could see her teeth, blackening against receding gums. I looked away, into the leaves. "But I'm not stupid and I'm not crazy." She shut her eyes but kept talking. "It's just that they expect me to say that I think I'm fat because they read that somewhere, you know? They believe what they read in books, like it's real. But I know what I am: I'm T-bone, the girl so skinny nobody wants to touch her. I'm just a twig."

She was quiet for a long while and I didn't say anything. Then, she turned on her side with her back to me, curled up, and went to sleep.

I couldn't move. I'd never had a girl lean against me like that: men, always, children, never. I watched her breathe.

With every inhalation her ribs strained, as if they would crack through her skin. I looked up into the leaves and grieved, for all sins against the flesh.

After that, I met Theresa every Monday, Wednesday and Friday for lunch in the park. She didn't eat anything, at first, but gradually she'd accept a scrap or two. I discovered that she was much more likely to take a leftover than a whole piece of food so I began to leave crusts, bones with meat still on them, half-drunk cups of milk. She'd snatch these up, her fingers bent like claws, and push them into her mouth, fast. I always looked away, to let her swallow in private; it was painful to watch her, anyway.

On and off, she told me a little about her life: she lived in a foster home; she went to school when she felt like it; she'd been told she was smart, could make something of herself, if she tried; she had a few friends; she loved Henry, her cat; she'd read all the Bronte novels; she was always cold. I told her a little about my life: I worked in a nice office; I had a nice apartment; I had read all the Pym novels; I liked to cook; I liked to eat; I was always a bit too warm. I didn't mention the men and, anyway, there hadn't been anyone after Dexter. I had, for some reason I still don't completely understand, decided to do without, for awhile. It occurred to me that I hadn't treated men as well as I maybe should. I was selfish; I'd used them for my own pleasure. I'd decided I needed to re-think men, when I had a chance. I mentioned that my landlady liked cats.

On Tuesdays, we weighed in together. I hovered around 210, seemingly stuck there. Theresa gained one pound, then two. Janet smiled on us kindly; if there were fangs and forked tongue slinking behind her lips, she kept them hidden. No need to gloat.

One day in mid-October, when the falling leaves kept burying my lunch, Theresa told me this story. I'll keep it brief because it's really too much to ask you to bear. When Theresa was five, she said, she shared a room with her sister, who was thirteen. The sister, naturally, barely tolerated her; Theresa was a pest, always getting into her sister's things, messing her stuff up. She didn't think her sister liked her at all. They shared a double bed and her sister slept soundly and silently every night, her back turned toward Theresa. She always stayed on the far edge of the mattress, worlds and worlds away. Theresa's father worked the three-to-midnight shift and when he came home, everyone in the house was asleep. He came, a few nights a week, to Theresa's room and he leaned over the bed, right over her sleeping sister, and he lifted Theresa up and carried her, still warm and sleepy, downstairs to the TV room, a room with a lock on the door.

I tried not to think about this too much but sometimes I couldn't help it: into my head would come the picture and I would see an even tinier Theresa, a Theresa just five, in pink feety pajamas, being carried away by that huge, silent man. And sometimes I could see it all from the point of view of that thirteen-year-old sister in the bed, that sister with her eyes clenched shut, not seeing, not seeing anything. Asleep.

When I was thirteen, I spent a lot of time in bed. The joints in my legs ached all the time and one doctor told my mother I might have some kind of juvenile arthritis and my mother fed me, as recommended, spoonfuls and spoonfuls of cod liver oil, supposedly to lubricate my joints. (I still can't eat an orange, the food she handed to me after the oil, to cut the taste.) Then another doctor, hearing this theory, snorted and said my joints hurt because I was so fat: all that weight was a strain on growing bones. My mother, in disgust with me, I think, gave up and left me alone.

So I remember being thirteen and left blessedly alone, lying on my stomach and letting my new breasts rub against the sheets. I would pull my nightgown up and let all of my naked flesh rest against the roughness of bleached cotton. At thirteen, I learned the pleasures of my own body; I learned that a certain motion, pulling my hips just right along the mattress, caused a weakness and sweetness to rush through me. I learned how to enjoy the weight of breast and thigh and hip pressing themselves down and down into the solid dark. I learned to see, as I can still see now, circles of light behind my eyelids, circles of moving light that tightened and loosened, faster and faster, as I came.

Afterwards I would lie on my back, looking up into the clear clean dark and I could feel myself riding the planet, moving through space. For a year or two, before I forgot how, I could actually perceive, I swear to you, the motions of the spheres. I really could; it's true.

I thought that I'd taught myself all that I would ever need to know about self-love, at thirteen. I knew that I had been blessed—grace, unasked for, sent my way. But I had to reconsider: maybe someone else, somewhere, paid for my grace? Maybe while, somewhere, one girl learns to love her flesh, another learns to loathe hers, to starve it and to punish it? And beside her, her sister wills herself to sleep very very soundly? Maybe.

Anyway, by the first week of November it was too cold to eat in the park, so I asked Theresa if she would come to my house for lunch. She hesitated but she said she'd come and then there she was sitting there in my kitchen, her black raincoat wrapped around her shoulders, held together in front by her two hands, fingers folded like amulets against her chest. She was so dark, a shadow in my yellow kitchen, and here, inside in the warmth of radiators, I could smell her, a bitter strange smell, like dry rot. She'd brought her cat Henry and he was sniffing around the apartment. Henry was an oddly-colored cat, light gray, solid, without a stripe. He was like mist, almost invisible in certain lights.

I'd stayed home from work, especially, to cook our lunch. My hands were warm from stirring saucepans; my face was flushed from steam. I'd made all of the things I like best when I'm scared, all the things I think of as nursery foods—creamed chicken, baking powder biscuits, graham cracker cream pie. Everything bland, smooth, almost colorless. Foods that roll down the throat easily, lovingly, without effort.

At first, Theresa stayed huddled in a chair but when I asked her to set the table she got up and did a lovely job, arranging things perfectly even while holding her raincoat shut with one hand. She placed each plate carefully, running a finger around the edges. "You've got pretty dishes," she said.

"Thanks." I didn't look up from dishing out the chicken. "I bought them for myself, when I realized I'd probably never get married. Gift from me to me. Here," I said, handing her a saucer of creamed chicken. "Give this to Henry."

She took the saucer in two hands, letting her coat fall open. Under it, she was wearing a heavy gray sweater and a black turtleneck and an old flannel shirt, layer above layer like a bag lady afraid to let go of anything she owns.

She put the saucer down and called Henry. He came right in, sniffed the dish and settled down to eat with intense concentration, tail wrapped tight around his butt.

I laughed. "Well, Henry likes it, anyway," I said. "Let's try it."

We sat down and I filled both our plates. I started to eat and Theresa, looking trapped, picked up her fork. She pushed chunks of chicken around the plate, just barely bringing drops of cream sauce to her lips on the tips of her fork. "It's good," she said politely.

I put my fork down, mid-bite, and looked at her. "Come on, T-bone," I said. "Let's quit bullshitting, okay?"

She put her fork down.

"I've got a deal for you, Theresa. Listen: just look at us. Look." I opened my arms wide, exposing myself and including her. "Look. I'm ridiculously fat and you're ridiculously skinny. Just look at us, Theresa."

She held her arms open, just like mine. She looked at us and then she nodded. "Yeah," she said. "So?"

"So let's swap. Here's the deal. I fill up one plate. Then I take one bite. Then you take one. Then I take one. Then you. Then me. Then you. When the plate's empty, that's it. I'm not allowed to refill it and you're not allowed to go throw up. I get thinner; you get fatter. What do you say? It's the only way I'll ever lose weight."

She looked at Henry, still crouched over his meal. "Can Henry live here?" she asked. "My foster mother hates him."

I nodded. "Okay."

"Can I come every day to see him?"

"If you want to. On Tuesdays, we'll weigh in."

She laughed. "That fucking Janet," she said. "She'll be pleased."

I nodded. "That's okay. She doesn't have much fun in life."

Theresa smiled, her gray, dingy, heartbreaking smile. "Okay," she said, and she opened her mouth like a little bird and waited for me to feed her. I took a bite of chicken first, then while I was still chewing I filled the fork again and lifted it to her waiting mouth. I watched her chew and swallow, my own lips and throat mimicking hers, willing the food into her body. Bite by tiny bite, we ate all the chicken on my plate, soothed by the richness of the cream. I buttered a biscuit and then I broke it with my hands into crumbs. I put a piece on my own tongue and she stuck out hers; I placed the crumbs there and watched her swallow each one. We drank milk from the same cup, in turn.

I've never nursed a baby and I probably never will, but right there I understood how it felt to present the breast and to feel it taken, to nourish a child right from myself: bone of my bone; flesh of my flesh.

Anyway, here it is mid-December and our lunches still take a very long time: they're slow and rich. Theresa still can't eat much at one time and I wait for her to catch up, swallow for swallow. By New Year's, I think she will be able to eat on her own, from her own plate and with her own fork. It will be time to wean her. I will have to buy myself some new year's clothes: smaller.

We've already bought Henry a Christmas present—a red collar with tiny silver bells. Despite the season, it reminds me of spring and it lets us know where that almost-invisible cat has gotten himself to, now that he roams free, inside and out, wherever he pleases.

Euclid Cooks

ROSIE'S EYES ARE RED AND SWOLLEN AND THEY BURN but she isn't crying and she doesn't rub them. She just lets the tears run. James says the tears will only salt the chili, anyway; he's the cook and he's being kind to her on her first day, she knows that. So she lets the tears fall, right off her cheeks into the pile of onion chunks on the cutting counter. Rosie is clumsy, cutting. She's slow; her onions are a mess.

James's onion, the one he demonstrated for her, sits just to her left, a perfect pile of neat white squares. James is watching her, quiet, standing off behind her left shoulder. He says, "No. Like this, Rosie." He moves up beside her, takes the knife from her hand and slices an onion into two perfectly balanced halves. "See?" He points the tip of the knife at an onion half and runs the point around and around its circles. "Look. Lovely concentric circles, predivided, precut. All neatly sectioned out by God. You just remember to cut across God's lines, okay? Like so." The knife flies like the blades of a fan and the onion halves seem to shiver themselves into sudden little cubes. When his onion settles, James hands Rosie the knife back, handle first, carefully. "You do it, sweetie," he says. He sits down on the high stool at the wooden counter and folds his hands around his knee, ready to be patient. His fingers are long and pale; he's wearing old jeans and a white t-shirt; his hair is blond and pulled straight back into a ponytail. He must be thirty-five, at least twice Rosie's age. He's the most beautiful man she's ever seen. She knows that he's gay, though, so that's okay.

She knows he's gay because he told her he was, about two seconds after she walked into her first day of work. "Hi, Rosie," he said, shaking her hand, which she knew was all clammy from the early morning chill and nervousness. But he didn't drop her soggy hand; he held it for a long enough minute to be friendly and he said, "I'm James, the cook, and I'm gay so you won't have to worry about that." His eyes looked kind. He had to look up at Rosie; most people do. She's 6'2" and probably still growing. "One thing off your list, okay? So this is the kitchen." And he showed her around the small cluttered kitchen, really just a kind of shack addition stuck on the back of the old hotel.

But it seems fine to Rosie—everything is scratched and dented and half worn out already, so how much harm can she do? Rosie takes an onion from the box and prepares to follow God's lines but when she peels the onion she gets the layers somehow wrong, so the surface is left all slimy and slippery and the blade edges off it, instead of striking through. Her hands are shaking and already her back hurts from bending over the counter, which would be high enough for any normal girl but is far too low for her.

James' hands swoop out over hers, grabbing the knife. "Watch it. Jesus. You'll lose a digit or two." He slides the slimy part off the onion and chops the rest, fast. He smiles up at her. "You'll learn." He wipes his hands on the corner of her long white apron. "I'll stop looking at you, okay? Just do the box of onions, then the bowl of garlic, then the celery and carrots, okay? Then the green peppers." He looks at her face as it registers the amount of stuff to be chopped. He laughs. "Yeah. Well, here at Uncle Bob's Gas Palace, we do need our veggies done early, don't we, love?" He moves to the old plush armchair over by the huge stove and sits down with a newspaper, cigarette, and a mug of tea.

So Rosie chops, slow and clumsy and bent funny at the waist. But she loves it already, her first real job. It isn't school and it isn't, thank God, home. The 7:30 sun comes sideways through the big dusty windows and lights the crescents of the blue bowls. The high-piled peppers shine like green lanterns, their scent strong, sharp. Soon, onion-tears flood Rosie's eyes again and little smeary rainbows fill her vision. She lets the tears run.

It isn't, of course, really Uncle Bob's Gas Palace. It's the old Stuyvesant Hotel, owned by Robert Davis. And it's not even really a hotel anymore, hasn't been for a very long time, sixty years at least. Now, in the one thousand, nine hundred and eighty-seventh year of our Lord, it's mostly just an empty wooden building on the edge of the Hudson River in Stuyvesant Falls, New York, Rosie's hometown, her only town, so far. The hotel's upper floors are pretty much scraped clean now, just bare boxes of rooms. The bar/restaurant is the only living part left, down here on the first floor. Rosie has passed this hotel on the school bus every day for her whole life. Every day that she went to school, anyway, before she quit last week. She's sixteen; it's legal. The only thing she thinks she might miss about school is Geometry, the one subject that always made sense.

James is whistling and stirring something into a pan

when she's done with the box of onions and her vision starts to clear. She wipes her eyes with her apron and the sunlight comes into focus again. The counter reacquires edges and the peppers shrink to proper size. The kitchen is getting warm. Rosie clears her throat. "I'm done with the onions," she says toward James.

He spins around, holding out a spoon coated with kind of creamy liquid. "Taste this," he says, jiggling the spoon. "Come on."

She doesn't know how to do that except by walking over, bending awkwardly down and licking the spoon, so she does. It's a strange taste, but what does she know? "It's good," she says, wiping her mouth on the apron corner.

"Good?" James's eyes open wide and he pretends shock. "Good? Sweetheart, this is my famous Cream Sherry Tarragon seafood sauce. People in the city paid megabucks to dunk dead fish is this sauce and you say 'good'? I'm crushed." He shakes his head and licks the rest of the spoon clean. "Sweetie, this sauce is superb."

Rosie isn't sure how much he's kidding, so she says, "It's probably very good. But I'm not used to good food. Really. I'm not. Should I start the garlic?"

"Sure. Garlic they'll appreciate. Garlic their gross tongues can actually perceive," James says. "Yes, do the garlic. We need lots and lots and lots of garlic. Today is chili day. Tomorrow," he says as he sinks back into his chair and picks up his paper, "tomorrow, God help me, is venison. The weekly Gas Palace Game Lunch, game, I understand, supplied by the Stuyvesant Falls rod and gun club. Barbarians." But in a minute he's back up, leaning on Rosie's counter, displaying a head of garlic. "Look. Now, here, the design is different. Garlic doesn't come with lines; it's not all marked and concentric, neat, like an onion. So it's a whole different chopping experience." He holds up the bulb of garlic and spins it in his long fingers. Then he drops it and grabs the knife, slamming it through the bulb. The garlic falls into two pieces and the smell rises. James points the knife tip at each half, where small creamy circles cluster around a tight center. "Look," James says. "Look at it. It's, well, oddly symmetric, isn't it? Like a flower, like a snow-flake, like, like a—what? Like a fucking fractal! Yes!"

Rosie isn't sure what a fractal is, but she laughs at James's excitement.

James grins. "But, that's not the best way to cut it, I'm afraid. Here, take each individual little clove and peel the sucker, like this." He slips the skin off a single clove. "Then just chop. No lines, no finesse." He chops, fast, and peels, fast, and in about five seconds, the whole bulb is minced, tiny. "Try it," he says.

Rosie tries. She can't even hold the knife over one small, shiny, slippery piece without sweating.

James moves away. "I can't look," he says, and goes back to his paper.

Left alone, Rosie can do it. It just takes her forever. But that's okay. She thinks that she's learning. And no one knows how strange and new this all really is to her; no one knows her mother. Well, all the local people think they know her, but James, at least, doesn't. He's only been here a month. So he probably doesn't know, yet, that Rosie is already firmly categorized as the semi-crazy daughter of a crazy mother. Every village has one crazy lady; it doesn't much matter how she gets crazy, but just that she is. Even now, when Rosie's mother doesn't even leave her house, doesn't go to work in the pie factory, doesn't stop people in front of the post office to warn them about the poisons she feels the world secreting like deadly sweat, even now she's a public figure, a kind of icon. Now she just stays closed in at home, wearing a surgical mask and filtering the air through the cheesecloth she's taped to the window screens. Rosie, folks say, is maybe only half-crazy, so far, just touched a little by her mother's contagion. And in any case, she has to go out into the dangerous world, has to work, has to take care of her mother. So she can't afford to be really crazy, but just so odd. So tall. And no one knows who her father is. Maybe Bigfoot, the kids in school used to say, or Lurch. No one knows that Rosie's mother doesn't allow any fresh food to come into her house. None. Rosie could shop twice a year and get what they need. Their potatoes are canned; their onions dehydrated; their milk is evaporated; their eggs, powdered. Processing, Rosie's mother thinks, may kill the worst poisons in the food. So this is a funny job for Rosie to have but it's one she knew she could get. Everyone knows that Mr. Davis gives jobs to young girls, especially young girls with little choice as to where they work, young girls who can't afford to quit. But the last one, the girl with the terrible burn scars, did finally quit, and Rosie took her place.

So here she is and, to her, the vegetables are wonderful. Feasts of color and smell, beautiful in the sun. Her eyes tear again and it's not from the garlic, which is done, at last. "Should I start the celery?" Rosie asks.

James has put down the paper, folded, on the counter beside her. He's looking down at it, while he measures flour into a bowl. "Four more," he says, nodding at the paper.

Rosie looks. "Four what?"

"Four more dead. Four people I know dead. Four friends of friends, dead." He shakes salt into the bowl.

Rosie moves over and reads the page he's got folded on top. It's a New York paper and it's the obituary page.

"Him. Him. Him. Him." James's floury finger jabs into four little squares of print, leaving four white smudges.

Rosie reads the names and ages. All were pretty young,

to die. Two died of AIDS, it says. One of pneumonia; one of cancer. Rosie thinks, suddenly, that maybe her mother is right. The world is sweating poison. But she still doesn't know what to say to James, who knows its victims. She feels herself, tall and awkward, hovering silent above the smudged page and she sees that she casts an unusually long shadow in the kitchen sunlight.

James looks up at her and smiles. "That's why I left," he says. "I thought I'd rather go before everyone was dead. Hand me the eggs, okay?"

The eggs are piled in a bowl, brown eggs, speckled with darker spots. The uneven, random spots make Rosie shiver; she remembers once, a long time ago, when she dropped one of the last fresh eggs to enter her mother's kitchen and it was full of spots of blood. She remembers how her mother screamed and how hard it was to get the bloody egg up off the floor. But this bowl is blue and the eggs in it look comfortable, like they're nesting in the sky.

"The eggs, kiddo," James says, pointing.

Rosie puts both hands on the edge of the bowl, wrapping her fingers tightly along its border. She doesn't lift the bowl, but slides it into James's reach. Nothing breaks.

James plucks up an egg and cracks it on the edge of his bowl, one-handed. The shell splits into two even pieces and egg falls gently, yolk intact, jiggling into the flour.

"Look," Rosie says, without even thinking, "it's two circles: a small yellow one with a diameter of one-half the big clear one." She points. "God's eyeball," she says.

James starts to laugh and cracks another egg, whose yolk lands just next to the first. "Now," he says, "it's two adjacent spherical objects. God's balls!"

"No," Rosie says. "God's breasts."

"Oh lord, a feminist. Okay, wait." James cracks two more eggs into the bowl and bows to Rosie. "There. God's balls and breasts. We've created an androgynous deity."

Rosie has no idea what that means but she's giggling so hard it doesn't matter.

James looks into the bowl. "But, shit. What am I supposed to make with four fucking eggs in it?"

"Double whatever it was? Or something else entirely?"

He laughs again. "Right. Okay, kiddo, so now it's not muffins, it's challah bread." He dumps more flour in and goes off to mix a package of yeast into some water. "So, you know how to knead dough?"

Of course she doesn't but by the time he's mixed it up and dragged out a bread board and put the round pale yellow lump of dough on it, she feels ready to try. He shows her how—lean into the dough with your palms, press against it, let it resist, slap it around, feel it grow smooth, watch it begin to respond, to push back, firm under your hands. The dough is alive and warm in Rosie's hands, lovely.

When she's done kneading, James lifts the dough from the board and puts it into the biggest blue bowl he's got. He sniffs at it and then laughs. "Uh oh. Strong whiff of garlic. You forgot to wash your hands."

Rosie drops her hands to the bottom of her apron and rolls them tightly in the hem. "Is it ruined?" Her mother would have had her wash her hands, hard, would have known that she carried something wrong on her fingers, would say that something wrong would come back to her, too, back from all those filthy raw eggs and nasty growing yeast. Her hands are sticky and pieces of dough are stuck beneath her nails, she can feel them.

"Oh, hell. No. Now it's—let's see. It's Garlic Challah, a bold new concept in Jewish/Italian cuisine. They'll love it." He covers the bowl with a clean white towel and sets it on the shelf above the stove. He looks at Rosie, standing with her long arms tight against her sides and her hands hidden in her apron. "Really, Rosie, it's okay. I should have reminded you. It's my fault. Forget it. On with your work." He holds up a piece of celery. "Let the lessons continue. Here we have parallel lines. And when you slice it—voila! Perfect crescents with nicely aligned holes where the lines bisect the curve. Look, Rosie. Even after you've sliced it all up, you could piece each stalk back together again by lining up the little holes. There's only one perfect match. Like the needle holes in Emily Dickinson's poems— 'Because I could not stop for death,' you know?"

Rosie doesn't know but she wants to get back in the spirit. She holds up a carrot and says, "Look, James. A cone. A three-dimensional form composed of circles of diminishing diameters, top to bottom." She moves the carrot up and down through the circle of her fingers, tightening and loosening her grip.

James rolls his eyes. "Stop that, Rosie. That's obscene." But he grins. "God's prick," he says.

So they're laughing when Mr. Davis opens the screen door and comes in. He stands by the doorway and says, "So, kitchen staff, what's so funny?"

James stops laughing. "Nothing, boss. Just stupid carrot tricks. Like on David Letterman, remember?" He goes to the stove and turns his back to Mr. Davis, stirring.

"Well, then, how's my new girl?" Mr. Davis, who is forty-five with pumped up muscles and whose head comes just to Rosie's shoulder, puts his hand on her back and runs it up and down, reaching to get to her neck. "How's little Rosie?"

"Fine," she says, looping her hands back into her apron. Everyone in town knows to keep their daughters out of Davis's reach. Everyone, of course, except Rosie's mother, who sees danger only in what she cannot see. Rosie keeps very still, even when Mr. Davis's hand slides under her shirt in the back. She needs a job.

But James turns around and says, "You wanted something, boss?"

Mr. Davis takes his hand off Rosie's skin. "Yeah. We need to talk." He nods his head toward the empty bar room.

James says, "Rosie, you punch down that bread dough, braid it up and put it in these pans, okay?" He smiles at her. "And wash your hands first, all right?"

Alone in the kitchen, Rosie scrubs her hands. Then she takes the heavy bowl from its shelf, cradles it in her arms and walks it to the table, where the bread board waits. James has oiled two loaf pans already. The dough has grown into a smooth yellow mound, perfectly curved and risen. James said "punch," and so she does, and the bread collapses with a sigh that sounds human. James said "braid," and so she does, cutting the dough into thirds first, then halving the thirds. She's figured it out—six even pieces for two loaves. She rolls each piece into a kind of rope and then lines them all up on the board. Her mother taught Rosie to braid when she was very small, and she'd braid her mother's hair when it was still red and long, falling over her bony back. Rosie would separate the soft hair into three sections, then weave them together, repeating her mother's instructions like a chant: right over the middle, left over the middle, right over the middle. She had done it for years and still does, every morning. Now her mother's hair is all speckled, white and red, and it is very very long, because cutting it, her mother says, could make her life leak out, but Rosie can still design it into a smooth, perfect braid. It works the same for bread and she can even close her eyes as she works. It's all known in the fingers, magic. She lifts the finished braids into their pans and carries them back to the warming shelf. She covers them again with the towel and goes back to her vegetables. But before she can even lift a pepper, Mr. Davis is back.

He puts his fingers on her waist. "James says you're doing just fine, Rosie," Mr. Davis says, twisting her apron ties, pulling the cloth tighter and tighter around her belly. "You'll stay right here, with the new cook. Don't you worry." He pats her butt, just once, then picks up a raw carrot and sticks it in his mouth, on his way out.

James is leaning in the doorway, watching. "Now that," he says, "is God's asshole."

"He said 'new cook,'" Rosie says.

James sits on the stool and starts chopping the carrots, smaller and smaller and smaller. "Yeah. I'm history here, Rosie." He laughs. "Damn short history, I must say. One frigging month."

Rosie takes some carrots and chops, too. "Why? You're a great cook."

"How do you know? You don't know about good food, remember?"

Rosie nods. "But I think you are. So why?"

"Oh, the word got out, that's all. I'm a hazard, sweetie. The local boys don't want their chili dished up by a faggot. I might spit in the pot, give them all the plague." The pile of carrots under James's knife grows higher, the pieces smaller.

"Do you have it?"

He laughs. "Nope. And ain't that a kick? I don't. Don't even test positive. Everyone I know, everyone I ever loved, everybody I ever fucked, they have it. Or they're dead. But I don't." He holds his hands out, dropping the knife. "Look, I'm clean. Shit, they want to test me, see why I don't have it. Maybe I am fucking immune. A jinx in reverse. Maybe I can't die, no matter what," he says, looking right up at Rosie, craning his neck to meet her eyes, "God's joke."

He stands up then and looks at the pile of carrot shreds

he's produced. "Oh, shit. Now we'll have to do carrot cake." He sweeps the orange pile into a bowl.

"When will you leave?" Rosie asks.

"Today's it, sweetie." He walks to the shelf and looks under the towel. He sees Rosie's braids, rising smooth and perfect. "Holy cow. These are gorgeous." He grins at Rosie. "You got magic hands, kiddo. Want a job in the city? We can start our own restaurant. We'll call it—what? The Geometry of Onions? What do you say? What should we call it?"

Rosie thinks about their restaurant just as if it could really happen, as if she could take her mother and James and herself, points on a swirling circle, and draw them into a safe center, where James's immunity would jinx her mother's poisons and her own hands would braid their lives smooth, once and for all. She believes it, for a minute, and the name comes. "Euclid Cooks," she says.

It isn't all that funny, but James puts his head down and laughs and laughs and laughs. "Listen, Rosie," he says, when he's finally stopped and wiped the tears from his cheeks. "I've got to make a few calls. I'll be back in half an hour and we will make the best fucking lunch this dump has ever seen." He goes to the door, but stops and says, "Cream sherry tarragon sole for us. Chili for the peasants. Garlic challah for all. Carrot cake with rum frosting. Lots of wine. Okay? Chop those peppers, now."

Rosie stands for a minute and looks around at her bright kitchen. There are the peppers left to do. Without James, she gets no instructions. She slices a pepper in half and it bleeds green juice on her hands. She is struck with its sharp smell and astonishing color. She is all alone and free to hold the pepper to her face and breathe. She closes her eyes and runs her tongue, just the tip, along the pepper's edges, tasting for once, the wetness of something perfectly fresh, unwashed, unsterilized, unfrozen, heated only by the sun. Her tongue moves over its surface, in and out of crevices, sliding along the slippery tight skin, dipping into the rich roughness inside. The seeds are tiny smooth bumps against her lips and even without looking she can tell that, here, there is a design not of lines or circles but of arches that lead to empty spaces, and beyond. It is not a pattern she's been taught. But God is in there somewhere—she has to believe that, doesn't she?

Learning to Bleed

I. Insulin

THINK OF ALL THE THINGS YOU WARN YOUR DAUGH-
TERS ABOUT—candy from strangers, busy roads,
bike riding without helmet, bad touch. Here's
something you just might neglect to mention: don't ever
let your best friend inject you with the insulin she uses every day to control her diabetes. I mean, really. Who would
even think of doing such a thing? Who could possibly imagine that two girls, best friends, would sit side by side on the
edge of a bed in safe suburban Scotch Plains, New Jersey,
in the hot summer of 1961, wearing nearly identical pairs
of shorts, and poise the needle-tipped syringe above their
thighs? Left thigh touching right, one tan and muscular,
hardened by needle holes, one soft, pale and unscarred, but
waiting for the shot.

Well, what can we ever really know about girls? Girls
aged eleven and twelve—how they feel about their best
friends, how they crave to actually be the other, how they

dress, walk, giggle, gesture alike. How they try to toss child-hood over their shoulders and how they march side by side into the dark maw of womanhood, attached at elbow, hip and thigh, until some razor-sharp edge of adult reality sepa-rates them, forever, with sudden letting of blood.

Is this exaggeration? I don't think so. When I was in sixth grade, the Stacy twins, Margie and Jeannie, and their respective best friends, whose names I can no longer recall, all sat down one bright spring afternoon in the Stacys' shady backyard and they carved, with a razor blade, their boy-friends' initials into their forearms. I wasn't there; I didn't see this act in its first bloody stages but I saw the wounds the next day in school and the thin white scars for two years thereafter. Think of it—four girls and not one skipped the second initial. Each girl carved into her own arm at least five or six deep lines. Every girl hurt herself that many times. And the boyfriends weren't the point; the girls' blood-bonding was. After all, the boyfriends changed many times over the years but those corporeal graphics remained forever.

Maybe those four women can still find those scars even now, if they run their fingers over arms grown slack and plump with middle age. Maybe, at night, lying beside fa-miliar snoring husbands, they turn their arms to the moon-light and, there, the totems of their foolish girlhoods catch the gleam and the women smile. Smile, that is, until they think of their own daughters.

But who could say to a daughter, "Please don't carve anyone's initials in your flesh, dear?" Even if you'd done it yourself, you wouldn't want to put that awful idea into words, repeat it, and perhaps perpetuate it.

And, really, given that sort of gory deed of girlhood soli-darity, the incident of Bev and me and the insulin seems fairly tame. Until you realize, as I did only very recently while reading a mystery, that insulin, injected into a healthy girl's body, is an instant and very certain means of death.

But, of course, we didn't know that. For three years, Bev and I lived next door to one another in large white brand-new houses on a street of large white brand-new houses. Bev was one year older than me but we did everything together. I stayed overnight in her house all the time, in summer. She never came to my house because her mother feared that she'd have a diabetic reaction in the night.

Bev had to stick to a strict diet to control her sugar; every afternoon at four, we broke apart one double popsicle, each taking one stick. We sat side by side on her porch, or mine, and sucked until our lips were numb. Afterwards, our mouths matched, tinted orange or garish green or, most satisfying, a deadly leaden blue. Otherwise, we weren't much alike, physically. Bev was strong and well-muscled, a much better runner than me. I was a head taller, thin and pale. I read all the books Bev never had time for; in neighborhood kickball games, she ran bases for me.

But still, we were best friends. So one July morning, after I'd spent the night and we'd played Monopoly until almost dawn, she said that I could see what it really felt like, her daily shot. Bev had just turned twelve and only then did her mother allow her to give herself the injections. Bev was proud of her skill and bravery. She'd let me watch, any number of times, and each time I saw her plunge that needle into her flesh, my own jumped. I'd rub the spot of blood away from her leg with alcohol, after the shot, and massage the sore muscle. Bev's thighs were lumpy and hard, scarred with dozens of miniature holes.

Bev was completely professional as she prepared my shot.

She chose a new needle and punctured the gray rubber top of a little insulin bottle. She drew the clear fluid up into the syringe and pushed a drop through to the tip of the needle. She tapped it to make sure there were no air bubbles. She soaked a cotton ball in alcohol and rubbed a cold circle onto my thigh. "Ready?" she said.

I nodded and closed my eyes, waiting for the sting.

"Oh shit," Bev said. "Wait a minute."

I opened my eyes.

She put the needle down on the bed, carefully. She bent over the night table drawer that held all her equipment, counting the little bottles in the box. "Shit," she said again. "Only six. If I use this one on you, I'll run out before the end of the week when Mom goes to the drug store. She'll kill me."

"Can't you just say you dropped a bottle and it broke?" I asked. I wanted, really wanted, to do this, to share this part of Bev's daily life.

She considered. "Yeah. But then she'd think I wasn't being careful and she'd start giving me my shots again." She sighed. "No. I better use this one for me."

So, just like that, my life was spared. We sat thigh to thigh and she let me wash her leg with alcohol and then she shoved the needle in. As usual, I felt her jolt of pain, but only secondhand.

II. Dolls

Bev's grandmother, Grandma Stoller, lived with her family. This was a trial. Grandma Stoller was a huge old German woman who spoke no English. She wore her white hair long, in a crown of braids, and she didn't much believe in bathing. Even worse, for Bev, was that she refused to wear bras. Her enormous breasts hung to the waists of her cotton summer housedresses and bobbled there like whales playing just below the surface of the sea. And still worse, her undershirts—the kind of white sleeveless vests that only men in America wore—were dried on the clothesline for everyone in the neighborhood to see. I tried to tell Bev that no one knew that those undershirts belonged to her grandmother, that they could easily have been her father's, but she was not comforted. How could she be? Her grandmother spoke in strange guttural outbursts, she smelled, she wore undershirts. She was every girl's nightmare. You can imagine.

I myself was terrified of Grandma Stoller. I never once saw her smile, she sounded just like the Nazis in all the war movies, and she had strict views on how girls should behave. She often yelled at us; it only made it worse that I couldn't understand what she was saying. I felt her anger and had no idea what I'd done to deserve it.

Both summers for the two years we'd been next door neighbors and best friends, Bev and I had constructed our own world in my basement. We'd hung sheets from the ceiling pipes to create rooms; we'd lugged down old furniture and rugs. We played an elaborate version of 'house' down there. We each had a certain number of dolls to serve as our children; we fantasized the husbands (and their professions) to complete our families. We spent whole days in that dark basement, avoiding the New Jersey heat and Grandma Stoller.

One day, shortly after the day I did not die of insulin injection, Bev was coming over, as usual, to play. She had two dolls cradled in her arms; she'd taken them home to make new outfits for them the night before. (We changed our children's clothes as we changed their names and sexes. One day I would have, say, two boys and a girl and Bev would have two girls; the next, I might only have one boy and Bev would be burdened with two sets of twins, mixed genders.) I was waiting on my porch and I saw Grandma Stoller step in front of Bev, blocking her path across my driveway. I couldn't understand her words but I saw Bev suddenly let the two dolls go limp, one hanging from each hand. Then she dropped them onto the grass and continued toward my house.

I watched as Grandma Stoller bent over the abandoned dolls and scooped them up in one large hand. She walked with the dolls to Bev's back door and she took the lid off one of the metal garbage cans that stood beside the door. She dropped the dolls in, one by one, and banged the lid down. Then she went into the house.

I felt how wide my eyes were as Bev came to sit next to me on the porch. I was shaking: two of our children, gone. But Bev shrugged. "She said that twelve-year-olds don't play with dolls. Dolls are for babies." She leaned over and scratched a bite on her ankle. "Maybe she's right. I'm sick of that stupid house game anyway."

I nodded. I didn't say that I was still only eleven.

We moved away from Scotch Plains a year and a half later and so I can't remember much else about Grandma Stoller except that I did see her again at Bev's funeral and she looked just the same, hugely braless in black silk. Bev died at twenty-four, from complications of diabetes, brought on, I'd heard, by the wild life she'd taken up as a teenager—drinking, drugs, sex, two miscarriages. This wild life began, presumably, after I'd moved away. I don't know. I wasn't there anymore and we were never big on letters.

But I did go to Bev's funeral, my year-old son on my hip. I shook hands with Grandma Stoller and I said, knowing that she would not understand me, "So, did she grow up fast enough for you, old woman?" I remember how Grandma Stoller reached out with a bent finger and touched my baby's cheek and how he began to howl.

III. Drowning

The last summer we spent together, when Bev was thirteen and I was twelve, our families joined a swim club and we rode our bikes there every sunny day. We didn't know, of course, that it would be our last summer as neighbors and best friends but even then, I think, the chinks between us were appearing. In early June, Bev had gotten her first period. I sat on her bed and watched her prepare the belt and pad apparatus that she would carry to the bathroom and strap between her legs. She'd begun to wear bras. My body was still as smooth and bloodless as it had been at three or eight, no sign of womanhood approaching.

At Willowwood, the swim club, Bev wore a two-piece bathing suit, daring in 1962. She didn't splash around in the shallow end of the pool with the kids. She started sitting with teenagers; they went behind the trees and smoked; the boys dove from the high board at the deep end of the pool and the girls watched them and cheered. Sometimes Bev and her girlfriends didn't even wear bathing suits or go in the water. Everyone knew that that was because they couldn't—because under their shorts, they were bleeding.

We always rode over together, our bike wheels spinning in tune over the hot sticky roads to the pool but once we'd arrived Bev wouldn't even sit with me. She'd moved on, into the ranks of the teenage girls, girls who'd stopped giggling and who strove to look bored. I stayed with the younger kids. Bev and I didn't talk about this; it was just done.

Usually, we arrived at the pool in the morning and returned home by late afternoon. In the last week of the summer, though, the week before Bev would begin high school, she asked her parents if she could stay later one night, stay until the pool closed at eight p.m. The older kids often hung around until eight, whispering into the dusk. Bev's parents said that, yes, just this once she could stay late, but only if I stayed too and we rode home, very carefully, together. My parents, always pretty laissez-faire, agreed. Looking back, I wonder why I agreed. I knew that Bev would ignore me for the whole evening; I knew that I would be bored and lonely. But I don't remember even thinking that I had a choice, really. We were still, in my heart, best friends.

That evening was hot and still. I'd been right, of course. Bev did ignore me and after all the younger kids left for home, I sat by myself at the edge of the shallow end, dangling my legs in the water. Bev and her friends spent a while watching some boys dive into the deep end and then they all, boys and girls alike, gathered into a laughing, teasing circle. They made a kind of tent of everyone's beach towels and disappeared under it. I thought I could hear Bev's voice once in a while, high-pitched and strange as she and the other girls shrieked at whatever the boys were doing to them under the towels.

By 7:30, the sky was still blue but the sun was gone. Mosquitoes began to bite my shoulders and neck. The pool was empty and quiet, as I'd never seen it, a serene turquoise jewel. I stood up and walked to the deep end, looking down. The black numbers on the side said "12 FEET."

I was bored and tired. I climbed the ladder to the diving board and walked out to the end, surprised at its ropy texture under my feet. I could swim perfectly well, but I'd never dived. Girls didn't, much.

I looked out over the clean, shining pool and decided, for no reason that I can remember, to jump in. I pointed my toes and entered the water like a blade; it felt wonderful to cut through like that. I remember smiling as I went down.

And I'm sure that what happened to me is very rare indeed. You would never think to warn your children: "Don't jump with pointed toes into a pool which has a drain with holes on the bottom because a toe will get caught and you will drown."

But, really, that's exactly what did happen, almost. The big toe on my right foot got stuck in one of the holes in the drain at the bottom of the pool. For a second, I didn't know what was holding me down, couldn't understand why I didn't buoy up to the surface. I just felt weighted, heavy and immobile. I don't remember being afraid.

I do remember looking up with a sense of pure amazement as my gaze traveled through more than six feet of clear blue water, straight up to the deeper blue of the sky. I watched as my hair floated in long strands above my face. My arms, terribly white and thin in the wavery light, stretched up and up. My fingers looked very far away.

I remember when the burning began in my chest and the sudden start of panic. I remember how all that blue light around me darkened as the capillaries in my eyes flooded. I remember, finally, pulling my hands down and folding into myself, wrapping my arms around my legs.

And that return to a fetal curve, I suppose, is what saved me. Once I stopped straining, pulling against that immovable drain, my toe simply came free and I popped to the surface like a cork. I remember that first breath of air and then floating on my back, gasping. The moon had risen and shone above me in the late summer sky, a thin copper crescent. Otherwise, everything was the same—Bev and her friends were still huddled under their towels and the night was undisturbed.

I climbed out of the pool, shivering, and limped toward my towel. When I sat down, I saw the blood oozing from my toe. Most of its skin was missing, stripped almost to the bone. It didn't hurt yet.

I wrapped my foot in the towel and sat still, waiting for Bev to come get me for the ride home. I was pretty sure that I could still pedal all right but I knew that I would be slow and that Bev would grow impatient and that she would go on ahead without me.

Body Snatchers:
the travel game

MY BROTHER IS BURIED IN AN UNMARKED GRAVE, somewhere near the New Jersey turnpike," Hope said. "No one in my family knows exactly where, except his wife — well, his widow — and she won't tell us." Neither of the young women in the car answered and Hope realized that it was probably an inappropriately heavy remark to drop into a silly car-game conversation devoted to strange disappearances, the kind you'd see on *Unsolved Mysteries*, where the missing are at least represented by live actors, bodily present and reassuringly solid.

She tried to make them see that it was funny, really. "But I think he'd be pleased, you know? He always joked about the turnpike, how they ran the road right over some of the cemeteries in New Jersey. When we were kids he'd bounce up in his seat in the car, whenever we rode on the turnpike, pretending we'd gone over a grave. He'd go 'Whoops! There's another one,' and bounce."

Hope turned her head to glance at Heather, in front, and Cree in back. They were both staring at her, not smiling. "Like this," Hope said, feeling a little desperate. She bounced, holding the wheel in both hands, and said, "Whoops! There's another one." She laughed, forgetting the girls and just liking the bouncing sensation, enjoying the memory of Bill doing it, all those years ago. She did it again, higher. "Whoops! That's a big one. That one feels like Jimmy Hoffa."

Heather smoothed her hands over her white shorts. "Was that your brother's name, Jimmy Hoffa?" she asked, still not smiling.

"Oh Jesus," Cree said, leaning up toward the front. She put her hands on the back of Heather's seat and Hope had to notice that her fingernails were painted black. And not even smooth black: sticky, flat black, like she'd dipped her fingers in tar. Heather leaned away, just a little closer to the door. "Jimmy Hoffa," Cree said, "was like famous. He was a gangster and they killed him and put him in the cement for the road. Jesus, Heather, don't you read?" She sat back, curling up the corner of the seat, clasping *The Vampire Lestat*, as if to prove her point. She added, "That's what makes it funny, dweeb. He's in the highway. He is the highway. Do you get it, yet?"

Heather looked out her window. "Thank you, Cree," she said, "for explaining that to me so clearly."

Cree laughed and went back to her book.

There she was again, submerging herself, Hope thought, in the world of endless nights and eternal darkness, where Lestat lived. That book had gotten them started, after all, on this disappearance thing—three strangers, stuck together in a Toyota for a day, trying to talk. No wonder it got weird.

Hope sighed, quietly. She never should have checked the ride board. It would have been easier to drive alone. It wasn't that far from Maine to Syracuse and she could afford the gas. But her old-time sixties ethics had kicked in, even now: if you're driving somewhere and you don't offer others a ride, you're hogging, somehow. Cars, gas, highways: they were supposed to be shared. And since it wasn't safe to pick up hitchhikers anymore, the student ride-board had seemed the next best thing. She'd almost forgotten, when she called the numbers she'd found there, that she was a middle-aged professor and they were likely to be very young students. And they were, both freshmen as it happened, and as unlike one another as Lestat, say, and Heidi.

Cree said she had no last name; she was an art major with buzz-cut orange hair and a pallor that had to be cultivated, Hope thought, glancing in the rearview mirror. It couldn't be natural. And it was highlighted by her all-black outfit — long turtleneck, tights, boots. Cree, apparently, did not acknowledge the arrival of spring; she was immune to May. Her entire going-home luggage was one steel box, stashed on the floor at her feet.

Heather was, Hope hadn't even needed to be told, an elementary education major. She looked like two-thirds of Hope's students — all those earnest young women whose names she could never remember until way after midterm because they all looked so much alike and because they never expressed an idea that differed, in any essential, from what they'd been taught by Mr. Rogers, right from their cradles. "I like you just the way you are," he'd told them and so they'd stayed that way, complacent and brimming with self-esteem. It was pleasant, being liked just the way they were, and they never ventured far from the neighborhood. They were emerging now, like some swarm of seventeen-year insects, to teach the next generation. They had smooth fair hair, round faces, and clear, untroubled eyes.

Hope was a little ashamed of her easy characterization of this girl, who was after all, a real human being and as such, entitled to as complex and interesting a life as she herself, but it was hard to imagine what form that life could take, since Heather had it all worked out so sensibly, already. She was nineteen and already engaged; she wore a small diamond ring and she was going home to her boyfriend, to whom, Hope had no doubt, she had been faithful, all through her freshman year. Her luggage was stuffed in the trunk, with the overflow tied onto the roof. Her one interesting item, a Habitrail cage holding twin beige hamsters, was on the back seat next to Cree. It sent out a warm, foresty odor which filled the car.

Cree nudged the cage with her boots, now and again, trying to rouse the hamsters, but they slept on, curled into twin lumps under their cedar shavings. Luckily, Cree didn't mind sharing her seat with them. "Rodents are cool," she'd said when she'd gotten into the car. "I respect vermin."

Hope had laughed, thinking it was wry joke. But Cree had been serious. "No," she said, "I do. Vermin have been around forever, you know. I think that they allow humans to share their space because we create so much garbage for them to eat. You know, crumbs and shit." She poked the Habitrail with a black nail. "Of course, these guys are sellouts, domesticated slaves and all. But they could break free, someday."

Heather had said, gently, "They're just hamsters. They don't want to be free. Their names are Bert and Ernie."

"Yeah, well," Cree said, curling herself into the corner, "even Ernie's got teeth."

And, with that, Hope had begun to drive. Now, three hours out of Maine, below and beyond Boston, heading west on the Mass Pike, conversation wasn't flowing a whole lot smoother. The radio in her car didn't work and whenever the silence deepened, she felt her thoughts pulled into the same old uneasiness: she was probably making a fool of herself, making this trip. Chasing after a man who hadn't even told her where he was going when he'd left, both of them furious and both of them in tears, almost a year ago. Not a word: he'd wanted to disappear and she was just too persistent and too well-trained in research to let him do it. She'd called graduate history programs in universities all over the country, asking if they had a teaching assistant named Rob Thornton. The secretaries were all helpful: when you sound appropriately officious and you say you're Professor So-and-So and you're looking for a former graduate student, something about a publication possibility for one of his papers, they just bend over backwards. Hope could hear them, over the phone, spinning rolodexes and flipping files. And, one day in January, a secretary had said, without even needing to flip, "Oh, yes, Rob's here. He teaches the introductory medieval section on Tuesday and Thursday at one. Shall I leave him a message for you?"

And Hope had simply hung up. But she'd known that he was at Syracuse and she had sent for their spring schedule and found his name on it and she learned that Syracuse's semester went one week longer than her own and she knew that if she got in her car and drove there, after her own grades were in and her office tidied for the summer, she could stand outside that classroom door and, at the end of the hour, he would walk out and see her there. And maybe he would forgive her, and hold out his arms. She wouldn't think any further than that.

These girls, she thought, are sensibly and sanely going home. I am going to make an utter ass of myself and I'm the one who's old enough to know better.

"Hey, you know what really makes people disappear?" Cree said, plopping Lestat down on top of the hamster cage. "I just realized." She sat up, hooking those fingernails over the back of Heather's seat.

Heather reached up and moved her hair just slightly to the right, away from Cree's hand. "What?" she said.

"It's time," Cree said. "You know, like a riddle." She seemed to search for a way to illustrate her revelation. "Take, like, your hands, okay? What happened to your little baby hands? I mean, think about it. Where's that whole baby? Where's that chubby little kid? Where's the kid you were in junior high? You know?" She tapped Hope's shoulder. "You know?"

Hope nodded and looked at her hands on the wheel. She tried to see the hands that used to be hers, from baby fat to teenage thin to young woman smooth. But she couldn't; she could only see these hands: square, small, dry-skinned, a little wrinkled, lines piled up around the knuckles, nails short, bereft of rings. The hands of a forty-two-year-old, her mother's hands, she thought, from the days when Hope used to watch her chop onions and knead bread and braid hair in their kitchen, thirty years ago. But now those hands had disappeared, too; now her mother's hands were brown-stained, swollen-knuckled, and they held, mostly, to the top of a walker. But her mother's hands, at least, still wore a wedding band and Hope had actually thrown hers away, quite a while back, tossing it into the same bag with the coffee grounds and eggshells. And she hadn't accepted Rob's offer to put a new one there; she could hardly remember why not. So Cree was right. It was time, and mistakes, that made people disappear.

Heather was holding out her own hands: lightly tanned, polished pink nails, sparkling engagement ring. She smiled at them. "Yes, they're different than they used to be," she said. "But all those other hands aren't gone, you know." She turned and looked back at Cree. "I mean, they're all in there, somewhere." She wiggled her fingers. "They just grew, that's all. They didn't disappear."

Cree leaned back, looking at her own hands. "No. If they don't exist, here and now, then they're gone." She made two fists and then loosened them. "They've disappeared."

Hope had a thought. "Could you paint them, though, Cree?" she asked. "Could you bring them back that way? In a drawing or a painting or something?"

Cree sat up again. "Yeah. Yeah, I could. I could kind of make them come back, couldn't I?" She leaned over and opened the steel box and started rummaging. She sat back up, a piece of charcoal and a small pad in her hand. She closed her eyes, for a minute, then opened them and began to draw.

Heather turned around, craning over the seat to watch. "But what about photos?" she said. "I mean, my mom has lots of photos of us when we were babies. Those exist, don't they? I mean, you don't need a drawing, do you, if there are photos?"

Cree looked up. "Listen, dweeb. What about the parts of your body that nobody ever took a picture of, okay? I mean, like your pussy, okay? Where's that sweet little hairless pussy, now?" She glared at Heather, who turned abruptly forward, facing front, her cheeks pink.

Cree poked her shoulder. "Come on, tell me. Where is that sweet little pink two-lip tulip now? Tell me."

Hope tried not to laugh. Heather looked silently out the window.

Cree giggled. "Don't worry, Heather," she said. "I'll draw one for you." And she did, filling her sketch pad with the hands and genitals of girl-children, in all combinations. Some had the hands just touching the genitals, some had the genitals engulfing the tiny hands, which were curled into fists. Cree kept holding up the pad for Hope to see, reversed in the rearview mirror. The drawings were certainly disturbing from that perspective. Heather would not look.

Hope said, after awhile, "What about people you haven't seen in ages, Cree? Could you draw them and bring them back? Or other people's lost friends? If I described my brother, let's say, could you draw him?"

Cree thought. "Like a police composite thing? No, I don't think so," she said. "I mean, I can't bring back your people, can I, if I don't really know them? Maybe I could bring back some of mine. But I don't know," she said, shrugging. "I'm not very good at whole figures yet, anyway. I only do parts."

And Hope remembered that this was just a girl, after all, a freshman, and not the miracle-worker she would need, to retrieve the bodies that were missing from her life.

When her neck and shoulders started to ache and she saw the sign for the next Burger King plaza, she said, "Let's stop, okay? I'm hungry." Both girls nodded and Cree tore off her sheet of drawing paper and folded it up on top of the Habitrail.

It was a relief to get out of the car. The air, even on the highway, was sweet with May. Even the Burger King was surrounded by beds of yellow tulips in bloom. Twin crabapple trees on either side of the entrance door were dropping pink petals and Hope watched while some caught in Cree's orange bristles of hair and sifted onto her shoulders, where they stuck. She looked oddly like a medieval bride, decked in blossom. Heather didn't collect petals; she was so smooth that they just slipped off.

Inside, Hope was surprised by their choices. Heather asked for only a salad and iced tea; Cree, whom she expected to be a vegetarian, ordered two bacon double cheeseburgers, large onion rings, and a Coke. Emboldened, Hope got herself a cheeseburger and coffee. At the table, Cree piled the onion rings onto her burger and then bit into it with savage delight. Heather's polite distaste was apparent, as she ate her lettuce and carrots with a fork.

Cree grinned around the roll. "This is how I acquire the spirits of my animal sisters and brothers," she said. "I eat their flesh while praying to be granted their wisdom. Sort of like Lestat." She chewed loudly.

Heather pointed with her fork. "Uh huh. Especially the spirit of the pig who created the bacon, right?"

Cree laughed. "Yeah. And the cows, too." She took a swallow of Coke and then started to moo, a startlingly loud and accurate moo.

Even Heather laughed. Suddenly they were both giggling like the little girls they weren't so far from being and Hope felt herself at a great distance. They could have been her daughters, silly, playful, beloved daughters. Perhaps that's how they appeared to other customers.

Heather stopped giggling first and said, "I'm sorry, Hope. We're probably embarrassing you."

Before Hope could answer, Cree said, "Oh, who gives a shit? No one knows Hope here, anyway. I mean, it's a fucking Burger King, all right? Who cares what anyone here thinks? We'll never see any of them again, right? They'll all disappear." She looked around for a minute, at the people eating at other tables. "I mean, we could be anybody, right?" She pointed at Heather. "Listen: we're just anybody. You can stop being a good, responsible student; Hope can stop being an uptight professor; and I," she grinned, "I can stop being so unbearably cool." She looked down at her hands and curled her fingers up, so that the nails weren't visible. "See? I could be anybody."

Heather nodded. "It's true—we'll never see these people again. But we can't really not be ourselves, I don't think. I mean, we just are what we are and..."

"Yeah, right," Cree said, "forever and fucking ever, ourselves." She uncurled her hands and spread them out on the table top. "And did you ever notice, when you're somewhere like this, that you keep thinking that you see someone you do know? Like that guy over there." She nodded toward a young man with straight blond hair, sitting alone. "I keep thinking that's a guy from my art history class. But it's not. You know, when you're someplace new, you still see the same old people for awhile, whether they're there or not."

Hope nodded. "Yes," she said. "And sometimes, when someone has left somewhere, and you haven't, you keep thinking you still see him all the time, too."

Heather looked down but Cree nodded, excited. "Yeah, yeah," she said. "Like at home, I keep thinking I see my mother, even though she left two years ago. I see a red-haired woman on the bus or in a store and for a minute I think it's her. All the time."

Heather's face registered instant sympathy. "Oh, Cree," she said. "Why did your mother leave?"

Cree shrugged. "Cause my father's a rotten, cheating bastard, I imagine," she said. She stood up, crumpling the burger wrappings onto the tray. "So let's go, okay? I want to get home and see the old bastard." She laughed at Heather's shocked face. "Well, he didn't cheat on me, did he? Just her. And he didn't leave, either."

While Hope was having the car filled up the girls stocked up on snacks from the machines: candy, gum, peanuts. When they came back, Cree had the blonde boy by the hand and Heather was walking at least six feet behind them. "Hey, Hope," Cree called out. "Get this. We started talking and I found out that Sam here is hitchhiking to Buffalo. We can take him halfway. Is this karma, or what?"

71

She stood next to Hope's window, grinning and holding onto Sam hopefully.

Hope looked up at his face: pale, slightly pimpled. He was wearing ordinary jeans and sneakers, a white t-shirt; he was carrying a backpack and a clarinet case. He certainly didn't look dangerous. "Okay," she said. "Get in."

"Cool. Thanks, Hope," Cree said. She opened the back door, bent over and turned the Habitrail sideways. "I hope you like rodents, Sam," she said, holding the door open for him.

Sam ducked into the seat and said, "Oh wow, hamsters. I had hamsters when I was a kid. They were named Bert and Ernie." He put his backpack and clarinet on the floor.

Cree nodded knowingly as she climbed into her side of the back seat. "Wow. That's amazing." She tapped Hope on the shoulder. "Karma," she whispered. "Kismet."

Heather slid into the front seat and slammed the door hard enough to express her disapproval. "You told him their names," she said. "I heard you."

Hope began to drive, feeling like the head of a large, strange family. Within five miles, they were all asleep: Cree curled into her corner, Sam with his head flung straight back on the seat, Heather with her head resting on the sweater she had folded neatly against the window. They are all absolutely vulnerable, Hope thought. I could cross lanes carelessly, make one small mistake, and not one of them would ever wake up. We could be hit head-on and disappear, all of us together, just like that. She kept both hands on the wheel, fighting sleepiness herself, allowing herself the pleasure of the slide into half-dream, half memory, where Rob was always waiting.

It really is the bodies, she thought, we miss the most: the particular fall of hair over the forehead, the sudden smile, the hollow in the throat, an episode of hands. When all of the reasons for not loving, for holding back, for failing in courage, when all of those have faded, it is the body we miss. Here, a year later, she could bring herself to tears just picturing his hands and so she stopped herself, afraid of losing her vision and killing these children who slept peacefully in her car. She sniffed, wiped her eyes on her sleeve and watched the Berkshires pass, white shadblow trees blooming in the woods, birches just now putting on their first bright green.

She began to recall her plan. She would go to Syracuse University admissions for a campus map; she would find the History Building; she would find room 302; she would stand outside its door and at 2:15, when the last of his students had filtered out, Rob would pick up his old black leather bookbag and he would walk out into the hall and he would see her. There, at that point, at 2:15 on a Thursday afternoon in May, Rob himself, in the flesh, became the variable she couldn't predict, certainly couldn't control. Had never been able to predict, really.

"So what was your brother's name?"

Hope jumped and saw Heather sitting up, facing front. She turned and looked at Hope. "If you don't mind talking about it," she added politely.

Hope shook her head. "No, I don't mind. I like to. My brother's name was Bill."

"And you really don't know where he's buried?" Heather's voice betrayed her incredulity. Clearly, in Heather's well-ordered world, you didn't misplace your dead.

"Well, no. Not exactly. He died very suddenly, unexpectedly, when he was just twenty-nine. His wife's family owned a burial plot in New Jersey and so that's where he went. My family was all spread out, mostly in California. I was in college in New Hampshire. I don't know, we just left him in New Jersey, like it was temporary or something."

She could see the disbelief in Heather's face and tried to explain. "Well, we had no family plot or anything. We moved all the time. We'd lived in New Jersey for a while and that's where Bill met his wife and that's where they lived. It seemed okay at the time. No one knew what else to do." She paused for breath, trying hard to remember that time, all the confusion. All she could really remember was Lou, Bill's young wife, crouched beside the coffin, combing his hair, trying to get it to look right. "Bill was only twenty-nine and he dropped dead of heart failure. Just like that."

"And, now," she went on, shaking herself into the present, "now, some twenty years later, my father, who now lives in Seattle, gets all bent out of shape and writes to my sister-in-law — who, of course, has remarried and has a nearly grown daughter — and says, 'Just where is Bill's grave, anyway?' And she writes back and says, basically, if you don't know, after twenty-six years, you don't deserve to know. She knows, she says, because she goes there all the time. And she's got it all worked out — she's going to be buried next to him when her time comes and then there will be a stone there, with both of their names."

Heather was quiet, looking out her window and then she said, "Won't her new husband mind?"

Hope shrugged. "I don't know. I've never met him. But the whole thing made my father furious and now he's trying, legally, to force her to let him put up a stone. The family's all divided over this thing; everyone is taking sides." Hope laughed. "Bill would think it was a riot — everyone trying to find him and him twenty-six years gone." She thought a minute. "Gone, now, almost as long as he was alive." She shook her head.

"Don't you want to find him?" Heather asked, still looking away.

Hope sighed. "Not really. I wrote to Lou, his wife, and said, 'You're right. Let the dead rest.'"

Heather turned her face toward Hope. There were tears on her face, running right down her perfect round cheeks. "But they won't rest sometimes," she said, rubbing her hands across her face.

Hope was too surprised to answer and Heather turned again and stared straight ahead, watching the road. "My sister doesn't rest, even though her grave is all taken care of," she said. "My parents go there every Sunday. She should rest, but she won't. She just won't give up."

"Give what up?" Hope said carefully.

"Oh, I don't know." Heather found a tissue in her sweater pocket and blew her nose. "Life, I guess. Me." She crumbled the tissue, then straightened it out, running it between two fingers, over and over again. "We were twins."

Hope felt her heart actually lurch. Twins, she thought. What could it be like to lose your twin?

"Yeah," Heather said. "Identical. Same hair, same hands, same skin — everything. She was older, by four minutes, that's all."

"How did she die?"

"She drowned. Two years ago. Her boyfriend took her out in a canoe, at our summer camp, and they capsized. She just sank like a stone, he said." Heather began to tear the tissue into tiny scraps. "It's funny, because we could swim. But the lake is really deep and really really cold, out in the middle like that. They didn't find her for three days."

She piled the tiny scraps into the palm of her left hand and began to pick them up and let them go out the window, one by one, with her right. "For those three days, you know, she was really gone. It was weird. Now," she said, "I feel like she's back, like she's still here, all around me." She let the last tissue scrap fly and brushed her hands on her knees. "Like when I'm brushing my hair or I see myself in a store window and for a minute I always think it's her, you know? I can't see myself without seeing her." She spread her hands out on the dashboard and looked at her ring. Suddenly she laughed. "You know, the guy I'm engaged to? It's her old boyfriend, the one in the canoe."

Hope's eyes left the road and she stared at Heather's ring. "Oh no," she said. "No."

Heather laughed again. "What the hell?" she said. "He said he couldn't live without her, he missed her so much. This way, he'll almost get her back, right?"

Hope couldn't speak. She couldn't even imagine what there was to say. She slowed the car for the toll booth at the end of the Mass Pike, where the Berkshires fell behind and the Catskills rose ahead. Cree and Sam stirred, in back, and Heather turned to Hope. She lowered her voice and said, "Don't tell them, okay? I never told anyone at school. The kids there think I'm just me, you know?"

Hope nodded, suddenly wondering if any of it were true.

Cree said, "Don't tell us what?"

Heather turned around and smiled over the seat back. "Don't tell them that while you were asleep we decided that you and Sam are an adorable couple and now we can say you slept together." She turned forward again and folded her hands in her lap, like a well-behaved child.

Cree shrugged. "So? I sleep with everybody." Sam laughed and Cree leaned forward, poking Hope's shoulder. "Don't you, Hope? I mean, don't you think we should sleep with people, a lot? While we have the chance? Before they disappear? I mean, what if we miss someone, before we really have to, you know? What if we have their body, right there, and we let it be snatched away, before we know how much we'll miss it?

Heather groaned. "What a crock," she said. "What an

excuse to be a slut."

Cree pushed her face between their shoulders, leaning right into the front seat. "No, this is not bullshit. I mean it. Listen: the Indians, you know, who used to live in these mountains, years ago, I think they're still here." She waved her hands toward the still-distant Catskills. "In spirit and all. But if I wanted to sleep with any of them, I couldn't. These guys," she gestured back at Sam, who was staring at her, "these guys are all I've got, in this lifetime. I don't want to miss anything." She sat back and started tearing up her drawing of little-girl parts, dropping the pieces into Bert and Ernie's cage through the little holes in the top. The hamsters didn't stir. She picked up the cage, swung it into her corner and slid over, nestling against Sam, who really had no choice except to put his arm around her. "So Hope," she said, "what do you think?"

It doesn't matter what I say, Hope thought, because I will probably never see these people again, and even if I do, all of us will have disappeared into different selves who have forgotten this whole conversation. Any of us can say anything at all. It can be a lie or the truth we're scared to tell anyone or both at once. To these strangers, we can say anything that comes into our heads. Suddenly, she loved them for that. "I hate to say it, Cree," she said, "but I have to agree. I have to admit that I have never regretted sleeping with anyone. I only regret letting one particular one go."

And Hope, driving into the movie-ending sunset, found herself telling them about Rob, realizing the sweet pleasure of saying his name aloud, letting it roll on her tongue, as if it were rightfully hers to taste and savor. They all sat up and listened, and they gave her advice, none of it more foolish than she'd have thought of herself. Some of it quite a bit better, and more comforting. She was cheered by their optimism. They believed that she could have him back, if she really really tried. Because he hadn't gone too far away yet and he must have known, they said, that she could find him, when she needed to.

Riverkeeper

ONE DAY, RIVERS BEGAN TO RUN ALL AROUND THE perimeters of Andrea's life. She met David and they went fly-fishing. He fished, wading waist-deep in amber water, casting the long green line in a series of arcs looping high against the backdrop of hemlocks and sky; she sat on rocky banks, looking, breathing, letting the sound of the stream slow her heartbeat and regulate her pulse.

Those were small rivers, the ones they fished, and they came and went in the pattern of days. An evening, perhaps, on the Battenkill, morning on the Esopus. But the Hudson between Stuyvesant and Albany was deep and steady, a daily presence. The Hudson ran on Andrea's left as she drove to David's apartment and on her right coming home. It was washed in sunset, going, and in darkness, coming home.

In one way or another, Andrea was startled by rivers every day lately, as if she'd just learned the word and up it popped everywhere. On T.V. in David's apartment, even, she'd seen a nature special called *Riverkeeper*. It seems that in England there is such a position. There are men whose profession is to keep a river. They nurture it like a fluid child, wayward, suckling, full of mystery. They devote their lives to the river which is in their charge and when they die they pass their river to the care of another keeper, a legacy. Riverkeeping is an honorable position, old, difficult, and all-engrossing, like motherhood.

Andrea had loved the program, which had even showed her the river from underneath, submerged cameras looking up at the surface. She'd been trying so hard, lately, to learn to look down into rivers properly, to acquire the fisherman's knack of penetrating the surface film, full of reflection and deception, to see the trout below. It was much more difficult than she'd expected. Sometimes a trout jumped inches from where she'd been staring and she never saw it until it broke the shining surface. And she never saw it again, once it was back below. And the show had taught her that eels in England migrate only during the dark of the moon, moving miles and miles through black water to breed in the sea. That seemed to Andrea like part of a witch's formula — wait for the dark of the moon, capture a swimming eel, boil with root of bergamot — but there it was on PBS, with the white-haired, kindly riverkeeper and his young assistant gathering in the eels by the basketful on the night without the moon. Perfectly respectable and real, after all.

Sometimes the moon would shine on the Hudson for her return trip from Albany. That lightened the trip a little, but coming home was still hard. She left David warm and sleepy in his bed and stepped out into chill nights. Her teenage sons were asleep in their beds, too, and she'd promised never to leave them alone for the whole night, so she drove back home, often the only human thing on the road beside the river. But the road was dense with animal life, swift creatures passing in front of her car almost out of headlight range, felt more than seen: possums, raccoons, rabbits, cats, deer, and, occasionally, the fox. One rainy night, a Biblical plague of frogs, tiny frogs leaping in waves across the wet road, heading for the river. She'd tried not to run over any of them but knew she'd killed many in her passage, for all her care. She'd shuddered all the way home.

Someday, she and David said, they'd be home together. But the time was not now, nor imminent. There were spouses, ex and not yet, on either side, children, in-laws, his dog, her cats. There were all the impediments to love in the ruins of younger loves; dreams were built on the eroded banks of earlier dreams, and she knew enough not to hope too much, or at least too obviously.

But at sunset, when he came back from seeing his little girl and called, she left her boys in Stuyvesant and drove joyfully north, the river on her left. She couldn't always see it behind the fields and trees but she knew where it was, in her bones. That May when she'd discovered riverkeepers, the sky was open and lit, the fields flat and full of flowers. The scents that rolled in through the open windows of the car were tangled and sweet. She put in a tape and sang along; she held a jar of phlox between her legs, nestled right up against her crotch, safe, not minding if a little water sloshed out onto her jeans. The jeans were old and soft; she'd lost weight, could wear her own children's cast-offs now, the boys' jeans and t-shirts, without a bra. She had felt her body grow younger in proportion to David's care of it. Even her periods were more regular than before, perfectly attuned to the lunar month. Twenty-eight days. Regular, persistent, insistent even. Twenty-eight days. Twenty-eight days. Now or never.

For rejuvenation must be temporary at forty. And she

was forty, her sons nearly grown. David was younger, his child just a baby. If, her tides suggested, this love goes away, the moon will set. Your body will wither, under the curse of the hag. Even now you are so thin that you are at risk, more boyish, less round. Breasts will fall, periods stop. If love goes this time. Now. Or never.

In the village of Castleton, halfway to Albany, the river suddenly became fully visible, running right along the main street. There it was, just behind the pharmacy and the bar, the Elks club and the Citgo station, just beyond the railroad tracks. Past the flashing light by the Stewarts shop, up the rise, the river seemed to grow huge, and just here, too, were the towers of Albany first visible. David lived just behind them and from here Andrea felt she could see him in his tiny apartment in a building full of people like himself, newly separated, suddenly alone, in transition. They moved in and out so quickly that the names on the mailboxes were never right. The first time she'd gone to visit, she'd had to ring every bell just to find David.

It was in Castleton that Andrea had first seen the deformed woman walking with her beautiful children. She seemed to have an apartment above the hardware store on the main street of the village. Andrea often passed the woman walking up and down the street, a baby in her arms, awkward, and a boy at her side, clinging to a leg. Andrea had slowed the car, caught by the sight. The woman's face was perfectly level and gray, as if her features had been modeled in clay and then pushed aside with the flat of the sculptor's hand, never painted or glazed. Her legs were the same putty color and greatly bowed, her gait rolling; her arms too seemed permanently bent, crooked around the child's round hips. She always had a cigarette in her mouth, smoke decorating the baby's curls. Both the baby and the little boy were strikingly lovely, with honey hair and syrup brown skin. Andrea was stunned by the contrast—the gnomelike mother, the angelic children. She had been watching them for many sunsets now, as she passed slowly through Castleton.

Sometimes Andrea even caught the woman's eye, she thought, although it was hard to tell from that flat face without movement or depth. But now and again she thought she saw the woman nod, a quick tucking down of the head, and once, for certain, she saw the little boy wave his fist in a practiced bye-bye as her car went by the light. Andrea felt oddly honored by their notice, a primitive thrill, as if she'd been touched by a family touched themselves by gods.

Then one day in the middle of May, when the sky was opening up more each evening, lasting longer and longer, fuller and fuller of promise, and Andrea had fresh flowers every night in her jar, she noticed that the deformed woman carried only one child. She had her baby in her arms, smoke clouding its head, but no toddler by her legs. She looked no different, otherwise, although it would be hard to tell. Her face was always blank, sand smooth, no messages written with sticks in its surface, washed clean of emotion. She just walked, as always, with the baby. But when Andrea slowed almost to a stop and nodded, and then waved, the woman stopped walking and turned toward the car. She stared at Andrea and then held the baby out, as far as she could with her bent arms, then gathered it back to her chest and cradled its head against her shoulder. Then she turned away and kept walking.

Every evening that week, as Andrea went to David, she watched for the woman and saw her with just the baby. The sturdy-legged golden-haired boy at her side was gone.

Just like that. Andrea couldn't bear it finally and stopped at the Stewarts to ask. She often stopped there anyway, as the weather grew warmer, to buy diet Coke for herself, creme soda for David, Pepsi and snacks for return treats for her boys. The counter was run by a middle-aged woman who looked as if she could be an old-fashioned postmistress, someone who knew the town's business, by heart.

The night was very hot for May. Andrea had to peel her back from the car seat and her shirt from her back as she walked into the store. She bought the sodas, then asked, "Who is the woman who walks with her kids through town? The one who's sort of odd-looking? But the children are beautiful."

The woman looked up from the cash register. She had a button pinned to her blue chest apron, a red drop of blood on a white ground. "I Gave," it read. "Odd-looking? Ruthie, I guess." She gave Andrea her change and put the cold bottles, already damp with condensation, into a brown paper bag. "Ruthie is her name. She showed up a couple of years back, already big in the belly. She lives right here on Main. Thanks, honey. You have a good night." She turned to fill the coffee machine.

Andrea stood with the cool bag held to her chest. The chill of it made her nipples rise under her t-shirt. She thought about David, waiting for her. He'd been so anxious lately. "But she had two children before. And now she only has one," she said. "And I wondered."

The woman turned back and pushed her gray hair away from her forehead. "Well, they took the oldest, I heard. Child welfare. He couldn't talk a word. Two years old and couldn't say Mama." She sighed. "Papa he wouldn't need, since there isn't any, but Mama he should know, by two."

Andrea pulled the bag tighter. The dampness from the bottles was soaking through the brown paper, wetting her skin. "But why couldn't he talk? He looked perfectly normal even though, she's, well, you know, odd."

The woman leaned across the counter, speaking low. "Honey, how could he talk? With a mother that can't form a single word? No father? No family? She lives like an animal, honey. I mean it. She can't take care of those kids. And God knows where she gets them." The woman stopped and began to wipe the counter with a cloth, looking down and then back up, flashing blue eyes at Andrea. "No one knows where she gets them."

"Well, they're hers, right? You said she was pregnant." Andrea felt compelled to defend the woman who had nodded to her. Those lovely children were surely hers, by right. Her poor cursed body had produced them somehow, against all the odds. "I mean, they are hers."

The woman dropped her cloth and put her hands to the small of her back, rubbing. "Of course they're hers. The question is, who's their daddy? Who around here would, you know, take advantage of that mute ugly thing like that? They asked, you know, time and again. Just asked her: who did this to you? But she can't say. Won't say." She leaned into the counter again and whispered. "And she cannot be allowed to keep them. She's not fit."

Andrea stepped back. The condensation ran between her breasts, down her ribs, stopped just at the waist of her jeans. "But they're so lovely," she said. "She seems to take good care of them."

The woman straightened. "For awhile, maybe. When they're small. But by two or three? Well, they have to learn to talk, right? She can't keep them, after two." She turned away. "Have a good night."

Andrea stood still. "And no one knows who the father

is?"

The woman spun, blood button bobbing on her chest. "It is none of our boys. None of ours, I'll tell you that." She walked through the door marked "Employees Only" behind the counter and left Andrea talking to air and bubbling coffee.

She walked back to car, got in, and drove to Albany, the river on her left. Her shirt was wet through and a tiny stream of water had slid beneath her jeans. She meant to tell David the story but then didn't. He'd had a rotten day; he missed his little girl. Soon, his wife was moving away, taking the child with her, and already he ached with loss. They made love carefully, holding each other as gently as fragile gifts, brought late to the party. He said once, looking straight into her eyes, "I may have to go with them, Andrea. I think I have to try."

She nodded, blank as washed sand.

On the way home, after midnight, the river rode to her right, full and ruffled. There were to be, the radio had said, two full moons that May. Two fulls on the ends of the month of May and the dark here in the center. An oddity, it happened only once every four or five years.

Here, Andrea thought, we are: the dark between two fulls and the next time will come too late. Just before Castleton, she stopped the car, caught by the scent of lilacs in the soft warm air. The bushes grew wild, huge, on the river bank just beyond the railroad tracks. She could pull her car behind the gas station by the marina and walk down the bank. She could pick armloads now, with no observers, and she could take some tomorrow to David. Lots and lots of lilacs. His apartment needed flowers to fill its transient air with smells of home. To convince him it was home, or could be.

Andrea left her headlights on, pointing toward the river, to light her way. She reached for the bushes; they grew high above her head and she could have picked all night without depleting their fecundity. She reached and pulled, raining dew over her arms and shoulders. She soaked herself with the lilacs, grateful for their unhusbanded abundance, this smell, gifts beyond deserving, grace. She filled her arms, finally, and turned to go. But she felt the pull of the river, black and deep beside her. The headlights lit a path, maybe twenty feet, into the water, as narrow as a candle in a cave. And there, just at the edge of the light, was the woman, deformed and mute. She was standing in the river, water massaging her waist, alone. Her skin shone white in the headlights and it took Andrea a minute to realize that she was naked.

Her back was turned to the bank and she stood straight, the bend in her legs invisible under the water, corrected, maybe, by the refraction of the river. Andrea, holding her lilacs, moved closer to the edge, held by the sight. She felt the pull of the current in her own dry thighs but held back, safe on the bank. Her sandals scratched the rocks.

The woman turned and looked at Andrea. Her shoulders tensed, as if to run, but she didn't. She looked at Andrea, no expression discernible on her flat pale face. Then she raised a hand and gestured — a simple wrist flick, language in any country. *Come in*, it said. *Join me.*

Andrea went one step forward. The water fluttered around her ankles. It felt warmer than the air, full of movement. The woman waved again: *Come in. Join me.* Andrea took another step and the river ran around her knees. She knew that this was silly, dangerous, rash, reckless. She knew better; she was forty years old; she was a mother; she'd taught her children better than this. But she took another step toward the silent stonelike figure.

Andrea thought now, in the wavering headlight beam, that she could see the woman smile. Her face was losing its frozen quality; the clay was warming, becoming flexible, giving.

Andrea felt her own resistance melt. She too was becoming liquid in the current. It feels so good, she thought, as the water rose to her thighs, pushing the fabric of her jeans against her. Her arms still full of lilacs, she stood, water pulling, woman pulling. The woman laughed then, a sound like a bell in the night. She walked toward Andrea, not pushing against the current but cutting it. She stopped a few feet in front of Andrea and gestured. Her arms spread wide in a tossing motion, her breasts trembling, full and round above the water: *Throw away the flowers.* Andrea did, letting the whole armload go. They were immediately caught in the river and taken away, their scent staying after only for a second. Their disappearance was magical, swift, complete.

Good. The woman nodded. Her hair was a ring of curls, damp and clinging. She moved one shoulder: *Let's go deeper.*

Andrea shook her head. "No." The current was very strong. She'd seen those lilacs go.

The woman shrugged. *So you're scared. Not me.* She turned and walked straight into the river, fast. Her breasts disappeared, then her shoulders, then her head.

Andrea waited until the woman's hair no longer floated on the surface. I can go home now, she thought. She has a right to do this, after all. They take away her children. Andrea turned back to the shore. But she heard the cry, the clearest ringing, and she had to look back.

The woman had surfaced, very near again. She was laughing or crying, her head thrown back to the water in a kind of hopeless ecstasy. Andrea could reach her if she would risk going deeper. She took two steps and the water became fierce, flattening her breasts against her ribs, throbbing along her spine, undermining her feet. She gasped and tried to back up but the current was solid against her and she could not move, could barely stand. She felt herself begin to slip and knew she would sink quickly: swift, sure, complete. It would be simple. She unlocked her leg muscles, opening herself up to a lover.

But the woman was right beside her, holding out a hand. Andrea took it and they stood face to face. Without effort, it seemed, the woman led her back close to shore, the water playful again around her knees. Andrea could stand and breathe. The woman dropped her hand and held up one finger: *One minute.* She backed up, into the river. Andrea, trembling now in her soaked clothes, watched her. She could sense the woman's nakedness below the water. She must, Andrea thought, she must be full of the river. It must have penetrated her like a man, right inside. It must be filling her, moving up and up. It must, by now, have found the womb. Andrea remembered the eels.

The woman, deep in the river, threw back her head and cried out, one sure shrill cry, as the river took her. Then she shook her curls, practical and complete, and walked out of the current. She came to Andrea and held out her arms, bent again, deformed still, and took Andrea into her grasp. Andrea's breasts, cold and shrunken inside her t-shirt, met the woman's, warm and full on her wry chest.

Holding together, they stepped out of the river, now passive, satisfied. On the shore, in the headlights, Andrea dripped and shivered. The woman turned and began to walk briskly away, still naked.

Andrea called out, "Are you all right? Will you be okay?"

The woman turned, crooked in the light. She gestured, her hands rounding out a huge belly in front of her. She gestured again: rocking a baby in her arms. She pointed at the river and at her shining, curling crotch. She smiled.

Andrea nodded and waved. "Yes," she said. "Goodbye. Good luck!"

The woman waved, turned away, walked just to the edge of the light. Then she spun back, transformed again. Andrea stared and flinched: the face was once again flat and unfathomable, a carved mask suspended on the borderline of darkness. The lips pulled back into a grotesque, two-dimensional witch's grin and she pointed a dripping finger, marking a straight line to Andrea's belly. *You too*, it said. *You. Too.*

Middle-Aged Martha Anne

Middle-aged, middle-aged Martha Anne
Lived alone in a frying pan.
'Til the cook threw in grease
And Martha slid to her release,
Never to be burned again, again,
Never to be burned again.

NONSENSE RHYMES WERE CONTINUALLY SPAWNED in Martha's brain, fidgeting there until she gave them voice and let them out. The only way to get rid of them, she knew by now, was to supply them with reasonable rhyme and some sort of rhythm, and then they would obligingly take form in the air and be gone.

So middle-aged Martha Anne, cooking bacon in her frying pan, sang her little song and then was free to eat her breakfast in something very much like peace. Her kitchen clock ticked earnestly, her tea kettle bubbled brightly. The late summer sun slanted across the table, tickling the edges of the asters in the vase. The air was full of lingering dew.

Back, Martha thought, in her olden days, she would have slept past the dew, dressed in alarm, gulped too-hot tea, and spilled herself upon the mercy of bus drivers in the rush to the office, where she could fall halfway back to sleep over television jingles and magazine ads, which she wrote. And rewrote and rewrote until their infantile strains had infected her dreams and impaired her ability to think in straightforward prose.

As who would want to anyway, day after day after day? Martha wondered as she washed her dishes in her awfulorange (one word, her own) sink. The house where she now lived, following her flight from her city townhouse and the world of work, was not what one would expect if one dreamt dreams of solitary retreats as rustic cabins upon isolated, flower-starred hills. There were no darkening pines, nor even crude water pumps to make the house romantic, the proper abode of a hermit or half-mad poet. It was just a small cheaply built house on the edge of a farm, originally meant to accommodate hired hands, whose hands were no longer needed, as so much of the farm had fallen away, field after field become house lots and developments and the farmer grown rich on harvests of banker's green. (Farmer, farmer, in the dell, haven't you done very well?) The hired man's house had, in earlier days, been lived in by countless restless workers, coming and going like breezes, each decorating bits and pieces of the house and leaving a cumulative design in walls of many colors.

Martha often wondered who had chosen the awfulorange sink and stove and refrigerator set and then who had capped them off with the brilliantly speckled magenta linoleum floor. When Martha redecorated the house she left the kitchen quite alone, a masterpiece of a sort, contenting herself with painting the living room walls ivory (in defiance of their previous puce) and her bedroom walls blue. Except for the bathroom, that's all there was to the house, and quite enough.

Martha had removed the plaster elves and lantern-bearing pickaninnies from the yard, but did not destroy them (for the good of humanity, as her son suggested) but allowed them to gambol for all time in the ripe darkness of the abandoned chicken shed, where she believed they spoke on Christmas Eve, although the substance of their conversation with the shades of departed hens was beyond even her imagining. The house, the yard, even the village to which they were attached by dint of postal obligation were, in short, absolutely tacky, and Martha loved them all, for she owed them nothing and they surrounded her with pleasant impersonality, a gift. She did not plan to leave them for a long while yet, despite Justin's constant pleas, calling often, asking her to come home. A kind man, her son, if a bit blind to his mother's needs, as who, all told, is not?

Dishes done (sparkling clean, shining like a dream), Martha donned her old woolen sweater for her walk into town for her mail and daily dram of groceries. The need for a sweater brought foreboding of fall and Martha shivered. Last winter the house had been more than a little cold, frost forming on the inside walls at night, for she had refused to listen to reason or neighborly advice and cover the outer window frames with opaque plastic, which might have kept a bit of winter out, but would surely have kept Martha in, unable to see outside at all. And she needed to see the bird feeders, to gauge their fullness and to watch the birds at their meals. Thirteen different varieties had come, on one glorious frostbitten morning last winter— first the plain brown sparrows, then the juncos and chickadees; soon titmice had come along, bringing with them the nuthatch and the finches, red, purple and yellow finches all aglow, lit along the sunflower feeders; the mourning doves squatted on the ground, catching drops, too placid to annoy the screaming jays, their blue like lightning on the snow. The evening grosbeaks joined in, brushing wings kindly with the unpopular starling and blackbird. Finally, like a benediction, like grace without prayer, came the cardinals. That day of riches still glowed in Martha's mind, whittling away winter's sharp edge.

And still, Martha thought as she started down the road, still it was quite warm yet, September just half over and the sun trailing summer behind it.

She strode quickly along, exercising her heart and lungs, if not her soul. At the dusty little post office the woman gave her her mail with a smile, mostly catalogs, some already full of a Christmas wares (toys and joys for girls and boys). She bought her supper needs at the grocery store where she chatted with the clerk, a lovely bald man with glasses and an undaunted ability to draw pleasure from each day's conversations about weather and gardens and such. Martha headed home, taking the long way, her contact with humankind done for this day, a contact small but satisfying, amply nourished by mutual interest in the commonplace. She looked forward to settling in at home with the catalogs, spying out all sorts of lovely things that she might order, for herself and Justin and Judith.

After lunch Martha would enjoy her nap, a tiny one, upright in the blue chair, a mere touch of sleep to give piquancy to an afternoon of wakefulness. Waking, she would garden, read, listen to the radio, and cook, if she felt like it. Late in the afternoon, on fine days, her landlord, the wealthy retired farmer, eighty-odd years old, would often visit and they would sit on the peeling porch and talk, or not, as they pleased. Mr. Bell would most often talk of days far gone and people whom Martha had never known but who had come to interest her, as tales of their lives drifted about her porch and lawn and settled in the window boxes among the impatiens. Nights, Martha watched *Mystery* or *Great Performances* on PBS, never daring to flick to other stations, where she might, God forbid, hear one of her own inane ads. She would sleep early, and well.

With this day all stretched before her, Martha walked home. On the final bit of the walk, she passed one of the farmer's last cornfields. The corn was her measure of time, more accurate than most. (Tick, tock, put in seeds; Tock tick, pull out weeds.) In May the field was brown sweet-smelling dirt. In June the new corn reached her knees, in July her waist, in August her shoulders, and now in September waved far above her head. In October it would become a field of stubble, studded with a few missed ears. Today the corn rustled with huge green energy, full of frantic whisperings and sighs. Martha quickened her steps just slightly and was bravely hurrying past the looming plants when she heard the cry from within the corn. (Tick tock, heart stops. Tock tick. Tock.)

She quashed her urge to run away and stood on the edge of the road, her ear bent to the inner green, and listened. The cry came again, high and pitiful. A cat, Martha thought in relief, just a cat. Here, Kitty, she called, bending at the very first line of stalks, peering into the corn, here, kitty, kitty, kitty. (Pussy cat, pussy cat, where have you been? I've been in a field, all green, all green. Pussy cat, pussy cat, what did you do? I trapped old ladies, all blue, all blue.) The cat's cry was momentarily silenced by Martha's voice but soon resumed, higher and more frantic, a plea from somewhere inside the corn.

All right, Martha thought, I'm coming, kitty. I'm coming. Martha was fond of cats and only did not own one because it was such a cliché for a middle-aged lady living alone to keep a cat and tell her friends endless stories of its adorable antics. The cat kept hollering, in hope now, and Martha blundered her way into the tall corn, pushing away the sharp-edged leaves that reached for her face and neck. The light in the corn was completely different from ordinary sunlight—pale green and full of floating specks. Martha felt choked and fought panic as she crashed about, calling, here, kitty. The cat's answer came back to her and she followed it as best she could without foundering among the protruding roots of the corn plants. She really did not wish to fall dead, to nourish this field with her fertile flesh. (I enjoyed the earth, now the earth's enjoying me.) She pleaded with the cat: Here, kitty, please come here, kitty.

The cat just kept on wailing and Martha just kept on blundering about until they found each other at last, clear on the far edge of the cornfield. (Martha, had she known, could have walked quite easily and safely around the field.) The cat's apparent obstinacy in not coming was made clear. Her leg was caught in a fox trap, the gray fur all crushed and bloody. Her yellow eyes made clear the fact that she'd felt herself doomed but now didn't, quite. Oh, poor kitty, Martha whispered, and then, city-bred Martha Anne, never having seen a fox trap (nor a fox, in a box), opened one with her bare hands and set free the cat, who could not walk and had to be carried quickly, wrapped in Martha's wool sweater. The crushed leg had begun to bleed heavily with the release of the pressure of the trap, and Martha ran home with her, crooning, poor poor kitty. She put her straight into the car, which luckily started after months of disuse, and drove to the nearest vet.

Who said he'd better put the cat to sleep and had Martha noticed the cat's pregnancy and what's more, advanced state of starvation? Unlikely to live or to produce quick kittens, at any rate. And Martha said no. Let's not kill this cat. Let's try to save her. And the vet said, who will pay for the surgery and Martha said, I will, and the cat's yellow eyes closed in anesthetic sleep as the vet removed her useless leg and she awoke in Martha's house in a box lined with baby blankets (twenty-five years old, from Justin's infancy and soft with many washings). The cat slept again and again, then woke to lap cream and then to stand on three legs as though she'd never had four. The cat obviously intended to live (one life gone but the beat goes on) and the kittens within, by their deep underskin movements, showed that they too scorned hunger and fox traps and the tricks of vets and were bound for life.

So Martha came to own a three-legged pregnant cat and was fond of its company in the little house and fed it prodigiously and watched its belly grow and shift in the sunlit mornings. Martha felt quite unalone and was surprised when Justin called on the phone in the last week of September, to ask how she was doing up there all by herself.

Just I, myself and me, a jolly noisy three, Martha thought but said, "I'm fine, Justin, just fine, and how are you and Judith?"

"Fine. Really great," answered Justin. "But I'd like to see you, Mom. I need to talk to you. Can I come up tomorrow?"

"Of course. Lovely. Yes, please do, Justin. I'll make a cheesecake."

The receiver down, Martha thought, dear dear, whatever will the man in the grocery think when I buy three packages of cream cheese, and after all the cream lately, too? He'll expect to see me grown fat as a balloon soon, she laughed. (Soon a balloon or was it buffoon?) She shrugged away her worry — she knew Justin would ask her to go home again and she would have to turn him down, again, that's all.

In the twittering fall evening, for the earth had now

turned away from summer, Martha lay in her bed and remembered Justin, her son. Not that she'd not seen him often, even since her move, but still she liked to remember. Her thoughts fled backward from the tall bearded man he was to the child he'd been and she stroked her memories as she did the cat. She saw again the awkward, trembly-souled teenager, the golden-haired boy with the baseball bat, the toddler with a rubber ball, the baby in the cradle. She caressed the memories no one else would ever carry, his father's memories gone into the grave. Martha's rubbed the cat's taut belly as her thoughts wandered and the cat slept soundly on the quilt beside her.

Oh, kitty, she thought, the tricks the world plays on mothers. Forcing us, beyond our power to resist, to love our children with an intensity we could hardly have dreamed of, before. And then to take them, by steps, away. If they die, as had Justin's infant sister, the loss tears apart our souls, our guts are almost burned away with the pain. If they live, we lose them still—lose the baby flesh whose smell was precious, lose the toddler curls that brushed our face as the small head rested on our shoulder, lose the sturdy bruised knees as they're forced into school pants, lose, eventually, the trust and finally the need. And the great grown son, the good successful man, is no recompense. None at all.

The cat, so full of its own impending children, had no answer and Martha felt comforted by the absolute lack of one. That Justin should care to see her would be enough. That Justin loved her she did not doubt. Her only living child, he had come to her without hesitation when her need was great, when Jack died and the terror of loneliness had battered her. That Jack should die, at fifty, falling flatly, untreatably, irrevocably dead upon the tweed carpet of his office, with Justin grown and gone, and leave Martha alone with nothing but the agency job and her vast and beautiful townhouse, was unthinkable. Martha could not have conceived it. When the flurry of women friends had subsided around her, their wave of support gone back to their living husbands and jobs and gracious homes (the homes requiring such care, these days, such exquisite nurturing care, more even than the children), Martha was left to spin in her own circles of despair. She could not be, alone, the Martha Anne she knew, the woman of means (her husband's), the woman of grace (her own), the woman of plenty (her son). She was falling, floating, when Justin came home.

Justin had come back to their townhouse, putting up, she was certain although he would never say so, with "Mama's boy" remarks from his fraternity brothers as he left the frat house. He had refilled her house with his presence. The bright rooms had lost the vast echoes and she had, once again, reason to put flowers on the breakfast table, and greens and holly on the mantel at Christmas.

Then, when Justin had married Judith, two springs ago (Justin and Judith and Jack, brought to you today by the letter J), Martha had left. She felt they needed privacy, and she felt, quite suddenly, that she didn't need them anymore. And she'd found this lovely-awful house, much to Justin's dismay, and lived in it, in singular unexpected peace. That's all, except for the family fiction, which was that middle-aged Martha Anne, in search of herself, had gone to follow her true talent as a writer, to forsake the ads and to WRITE, in capital letters. That she hadn't put pen to paper in over a year did not dispute the idea, for no one knew it but Martha herself, who had no intention of writing anything, ever. But let them think so, an easy explanation. Martha Anne shifted onto her side in bed, and slept.

At 11:15 the next morning, Justin arrived and Martha held him tightly in her arms, enclosing for a moment the infant and the child and the man as best she could. They sat down to cheesecake and coffee and talk. Or really, Justin talked, seeming to have memorized his little speech on the highway. "Mom, I have great news." His eyes asked her to think it great. "Judith's pregnant. And, Mom, we really want you to come home now. Listen, we've thought it all out. We can fix up the top floor of the house into an apartment. You'll have all the privacy you need. We've already started to put a kitchen up there. A very nice one." He just avoided shuddering at the kitchen in which they sat.

"Judith is going to keep on at school, Mom, right up until the baby comes, studying to pass the bar. And, after, well, we know she'll find a place in a good firm and we'll have plenty of money for sitters, and you'll be free to be with the baby, but you'll have plenty of time to write too, and...." Justin's breath finally collapsed and he looked at Martha quietly. "We'd like you to come home."

Martha felt betrayed by her instantly filled eyes. She fiddled with the coffee pot before speaking. "Justin, that's wonderful news. A grandchild! How lovely. How grand! But, still, I thought I'd stay here for awhile, you know, finish my book (liar, liar, pants on fire). And I'd hate to move the cat now, and all," she ended limply.

"Oh come on, Mom, the cat? We'll bring the damn cat. Last year it was the birds. Remember? Here it was fifty degrees in this shack and you wouldn't leave because the birds would die if you didn't keep filling the feeders. Remember? Honest to God, Mom, birds, cats, babies, are they all the same to you?" Justin's face was dark and pressing.

Martha sighed, acknowledging his point. "No, of course not. It's just that, you know," and here Martha spoke more truthfully than was her wont with Justin," you know, there is nothing so despised on earth as pregnant cats and middle-aged women. I just think we should stick together, that's all." She tried a smile.

"Mom." Justin's voice was full of compassion hovering just above annoyance. "That's a crock. You're not despised, you're wanted. We really want you, Judith and I. And the baby, think how the baby will want you."

The baby, a baby with a mother in a law firm, a baby with no one to cherish and preserve in memory all the days of its small and singular life. Martha's eyes betrayed her again, but she tried to rally. "Justin, I just don't know. I'm happy here, you know."

Justin stood up, clearly hurt. "Judith and I are happy, too. We just thought that maybe we could all be happy together. I respect your work, but I just can't believe you have to be all alone in some godforsaken place to do it."

Her work. Martha had no reply, nothing at all to answer her son.

Justin bent then and kissed the top of her head. "I'll call soon. You think about it."

Martha, looking at her magnificent magenta floor, asked, "Give me a month, all right? One month to decide." She felt Justin's smile and knew that he was quite sure of her now.

"Sure, Mom, a month is fine. The baby's not due until after Christmas anyway." He laughed and said shyly, "We'd like you to help us with names—with your imagination I know you'll come up with something great."

When he left, he walked with the long strides of his father in the past and his child in the future. He carries it all within him, Martha thought, watching him through a cracked pane. She was hardly necessary to all that now, was she?

In about a month, Martha thought, the corn would be

chopped and the leaves gone from the trees. She hadn't yet begun to feed the birds.

Deep in the night, the cat gave birth. Martha awoke to a pained mewing and arose to watch as the cat labored in the box. She shivered in her flannel nightgown beside the small drama and watched each kitten arrive, wet and smelling deeply of blood and birth. There were eventually four, all the same undistinguished gray as their mother. They mewled about, then found the cat's nipples and gave suck, strong and healthy. The cat purred and licked.

Martha finally found the courage to dislodge one of the tiny beasts from its mother's breast, and she held it against her cheek, breathing in its odor of life. It struggled and cried, and alarm sprang into the cat's yellow eyes, so Martha returned it, safe, to the soft nest of Justin's baby blankets.

> Pussy cat, pussy cat, where have you been?
> I've been to London. I've been a queen.
> Pussy cat, pussy cat, that is not true.
> I've been a queen, I say. Have you?

Ashes

MAY SHIFTED THE BACKPACK WITH A SHOULDER shrug. She couldn't use her hands without letting go of the reins. If she let go of the reins, the mule would run or buck or stop suddenly or something and, in any one of those cases, send her flying into the Grand Canyon. The pack was heavy. She was sweaty. Her legs were too short for the stirrups, even though the guide had pulled and cinched, shortening them as short as they would go. Her feet, in size 4 hiking boots, not easy to find, just touched the opening of the stirrups and she had to keep her toes pointed, constantly stretching her leg muscles. *En* fucking *pointe*, in hiking boots on the back of a mule in the middle of summer in the Grand Canyon. She shifted her neck. The pack rubbed, just there, on her left shoulder blade, somewhere near the backside of her heart.

John was careful about creating fire in his kitchen. He had spread a sheet of aluminum foil in the sink first, shaping it around the corners with his fingertips. There could be no scorch marks: Jill would surely notice any burnt places in her sink when she came home later and washed the baby's supper dish.

The foil felt much cooler than the summer air, air thick with thunder, calling, rolling toward the valley the way it always did. The thunder had more to do with John's decision to burn the letter than he'd have let on. It had brought with it a kind of atavistic fear—premonitions, dreams recalled.

He took the sheets from the envelope. Only two sheets but heavy with type. No perfume, no flowery writing, no signature. Just fine gray paper with honest gray type. Line after line of it, speaking of love and joy and possibility. Hope, that thing with feathers, new again and ready to fly.

He laid the two pages on the foil in order and read them over, the matches on the counter. He knew them perfectly well anyway, even though the letter had arrived just that morning in the hours of sun before the storm. He would swear that the clouds appeared in the west, piled like mountains on top of mountains, the minute he walked out of the post office. He knew that he had a tendency to read signs in nothing and portents in bare air but surely it was significant that he entered the post office in sun and came out into that strange green light that always carries the weight of imminent rain, thunder on its back. His pocket had grown heavy with the dove-gray envelope. It unbalanced him, pitching his gait forward like a woman full of child.

Anne rode up beside May. Her face was sweaty under her Ranger Rick hat but she was grinning, looking unburdened. Of course, she didn't have a six-ton pack pulling her to earth.

"Hey, kiddo," Anne said. "How are you bearing up under the weight of the world's sorrow?"

"Fuck off, Anne." May slid her shoulders around, trying to move the straps out of the ruts they were digging in her flesh. "This thing really hurts."

Anne nodded. "I bet it does. Listen, you know I'll take it for a while if you want me to."

May looked over at Anne, who rode easy in her saddle. Anne, her best friend, her department colleague, her helpmate, but not, quite, her confidante, at least not about matters May feared might be unforgivable, between women. Anne was tall and thin and graceful; her feet reached the stirrups. Anne was always centered; her feet always touched ground. Only May bounced along somewhere above it, levitated by dreams, ideas, ridiculous enthusiasms, mistakes of grand proportion. She sighed. "No. It's okay."

Their mules walked in swaying tandem on the trail, going down and down into the glistening heat. Always down. Abandon hope. "I think it's permanently embedded in my back, anyway," May said. "It has taken possession of my spinal cord, my entire central nervous system. I'm completely at its mercy." She smiled, as if she were joking.

Anne didn't smile back. "You really do look shitty. You're all white and clammy. I told you not to do this."

"Oh, Christ. I know. You told me. And told me. It's my own damn business."

"And if you die of exhaustion in this canyon, whose business then?" Anne's face was shaded by her hat but May could see the flash of her eyes.

"You don't die, Anne. Remember, nothing is ever as bad as it seems. You hardly ever die of things." May stretched her neck, pulling away from the pack. It was very hot on her back. Sweat kept pooling under it and then running down her back in little streams that met and coursed together in the center, dripping down her spine. She thought of the tiny river that had carved the Canyon, eating away at so so solid earth over the centuries. Her back was eroding much more quickly.

Anne snorted, surprising both mules, whose ears turned backwards as if to pick up any other interesting human signals. "You just don't take on the weight of everybody's heartaches without paying a price, May. You don't offer to carry all the ashes of all the pains of all your friends into the Grand Canyon to bury them. Not without paying, you don't. You don't become the savior without the cross. Did you think it would be light, a sack of ashes?"

"It's only a goddamn Smucker's jar, Anne." May shook her right arm, still clinging to the reins, then her left. "All the ashes from everybody in our department fit into one Smucker's Grape Jelly jar, the twelve-ounce size. It was amazing." She tried to picture them coming, one by one, with little bits of ash in envelopes. She'd announced it at their last department meeting of the spring: she was going to the Grand Canyon over the summer and she'd decided to bury some shit there. She'd told them how. Write on a piece of paper some sorrow, some negative something, some private pain. Something you want out of your life. Then burn the paper and bring me the ashes. I'll take them all to the fucking Grand fucking Canyon and bury them there at the bottom. And then I'll plant some sunflower seeds around the grave.

Funny that no one laughed. She'd expected them to laugh but they just cleared throats. Then someone mentioned that they'd read that the burying of obsessive thoughts was an established treatment for victims of obsessive/compulsive disorder, that primitive peoples and children often believed that if something was burned, it was magically and truly gone. Someone else brought up

Faulkner, *As I Lay Dying*, Cash's wish for a clean flame for his mother's rotting body. Instead of dragging it all over the countryside in that Mississippi July heat—a clean flame. But someone else said, "Yeah, but when the barn did burn, Cash took the coffin out. He couldn't let it burn because he'd built it himself, with beveled edges." Someone else sighed and the chair said, "Well. Our next agenda item concerns the retirement dinner for...."

But it appeared on the minutes, item 8: "See May about ash disposal in f-G. f-C."

And they'd come, at least some of them, and slipped envelopes under her door, sliding them in where she'd find them, first thing in the mornings. And when she'd emptied them, with proper delicacy and respect, into a blue coffee mug, the ashes seemed pitifully small for the pains of so many people. Even when she'd added her own, which of course to her felt enormous, the remains of pages and pages of frantic confession—"I slept with a man when his wife was pregnant, when she was in labor, even. Unforgivable, unforgivable."—burnt in her metal office wastebasket, the whole batch had poured easily into the twelve-ounce Smucker's jar, the one with the purple and white checkered top. It didn't weigh a thing, after all.

Anne sighed. "Remember that old story about this very strong, enormous guy who carries a strange man on his back across a river? Just a skinny-ass Smucker's-size stranger, but the muscle guy can hardly lift him and he gets heavier and heavier and finally when they stagger to the other side, the skinny guy climbs off and the muscle guy collapses. And the strong guy says, 'Goddamn, you're heavy, man,' and the other guy smiles this skinny beatific smile and says, 'My name is Jesus and I bear the weight of the world.'" Anne glared. "Remember that one, May?"

May laughed. "It's coming back to me. Was that Saint

Christopher?"

"How the hell should I know? The point is ...."

"I get the point, Anne. Sorrow is heavy even if the jar ain't. I'm learning."

"So, do you want me to take it for awhile?"

May considered. It was dreadfully hot. "No. It's my job. You didn't even contribute any ashes. At least you said you didn't."

"I didn't. I'm not stupid enough to think you can burn up pain."

"Oh come off it. What else can you do with it? You just ...."

A guide's voice sang out, sickeningly chipper in the arid air, "Single file here, ladies. The trail narrows and steepens here. Single file, please."

May's mule immediately dropped behind Anne's. The mules knew the trail. Or maybe, May thought, her mule was just getting tired, thinking, Goddamn, you're heavy, lady. But, mulelike, it plodded on, deeper and deeper into the heat.

John lit the pages at all four corners, one at a time, moving clockwise. The envelope, as well. The paper was good, heavy and smooth. It took some time to catch and when it did, burned slowly. He tried to watch the order of the words as they were consumed, guessing which would be last. It would be nice if "love" were there at the end, glowing up through the ash. But she'd only used "love" three times and they were sprinkled about the paper in odd spots, top and bottom, so they burnt quickly as the pages crimped from the edges in. There was no order, no omen, no sign in the pattern of disappearance, at least not one John could determine. The words just went quietly into the flame as it spread from the corners in. Even when the words were gone, the paper held together, dark and frail. It had been good paper, substantial and weighty.

The temperature went ten degrees up for each fifteen feet down. Isn't that what the guides had said? Each step of the mule a fraction of a degree hotter.

But not to worry, they'd added. The temperature at the floor of the Canyon is always about the same as in Phoenix, Arizona, which lies at the same level. Both equally hot—sea level without the blessing of the sea. And people live in Phoenix, all the time. So May believed. She'd never been there and wasn't going. This was enough.

May was staring into Anne's mule's behind. She concentrated on its dusty buttocks, trying to decide if that was the proper thing to call them. Do mules have buttocks, technically? Does anything that doesn't sit need buttocks, really? Still, they moved in a steady, soporific rhythm: left muscles bunched, then long; right bunched, then long; left again. Down. May considered sleeping, but only with her eyes open. You must look at life, she believed, stare at where you're going. Sometimes it's the only virtue left. At least you can always say, afterwards, that you didn't hide your eyes.

The back of even Anne's shirt was stained now, damp with patches of sweat. May could just imagine what her own back must look like to the guy behind her, like it was on fire. Not flames, but the slow deep glow of ashes left overnight in the stove, ready to catch the morning's kindling.

That's it, she thought. Some jerk left the fire in his or her ashes. Someone's never went out. Some one of her fine Ph.D.-holding friends without a rat's ass worth of common sense gave her ashes still on fire, for Christ's sake. And now they were catching again, taking fuel from someone else's unconsumed pain. Jesus.

When it was done, John crimped the foil into a very small ball. He placed it in the garbage bag under the sink, where it settled, indistinguishable from the other discards. He rinsed the sink. He smelled the air. There was a lingering trace of smoke but it would be gone by the time Jill got home. "There," he said, nodding in the direction of their bedroom, "did I do it right?"

He wasn't, as one might think, addressing the innocence of their conjugal bed. He was addressing the dream he'd dreamt there two nights before, the warning. Sometimes, you cannot not pay attention to dreams.

The heat was so searing that they must be near the bottom, May thought. And there was something even to be said for that, supposedly. Once you hit bottom, the therapist-types like to say, then you can start back up. But not before.

But it wasn't as easy as May had thought, giving up. You couldn't just sink to the bottom, weighted by gravity and contrition. You had to plod there, one small mule-step at a time, like in some awful slow-motion nightmare. It was work, a labor, and one with no child at its end.

And, besides, she was cheating and she knew it. She'd written him one more letter. Just one, just in case. Hedging her bets, as always.

It was the kind of a dream that John had often, but never

told anyone about. He hated people who told you their dreams, anyway. Dreams are private conversations with the cosmos. Dreams, like letters, are meant for only one set of eyes. In the dream, he was always walking or driving, or both, down a road strewn with fallen branches. It was always just after a storm, with the thunder and lightning over, when the world seemed again safe. The sky was always that vivid post-rain blue, the air sweet, leaves intensely green.

In this version of the dream, he was talking on the phone while he walked. Talking to his dissertation director, a woman he hadn't seen in years. She was saying, "Are you out walking in this mess, John? Aren't there branches and wires down all over?"

He answered lightly. He was always light-hearted in the dream, happy, free. "It's nothing. The storm's over."

The phone disappeared and he saw the black wire on the ground in front of him. That was the important part: he saw it and he stepped on it anyway. Just like that. Put his foot squarely on it and felt the first surge of current running lightly along his muscles, touching, playing a sensuous game that brought a lovely heaviness to his limbs, like that sweet sweet weakness before sex. The power grew and he thought, "What a story this will make, tomorrow. I'll call her tomorrow and tell her how I stepped on this wire and its power just about knocked me out, like she does."

But he stopped thinking about the story he would tell her when it started to hurt. The pain grew. It hurt very very badly: a pain that flamed along every part of his body, rushing along the charged nerves. He could not take his foot off the wire; he hadn't the strength to save himself. The hair on his arms was scorching; he felt his eardrums burst.

By the time they reached the level of the sea and Phoenix, the temperature in both was 121 degrees. The guides said they wouldn't be able to stay long, because of that, but to find a bit of shade, if possible, and to drink water, lots of it.

Anne held the cup to May's mouth but she couldn't drink. Her throat was as closed as her back was opened. She whispered. "No. Let's just bury this shit."

So they wandered off, away from the exhausted little clump of intrepid tourists, the one percent that make it as far as the canyon floor. They followed the river down and found a spot. It was nothing special, just a kind of notch near the wall.

May knelt, leaning her forehead against the rocks.

"God," Anne said. "You look like you're at the Wailing Wall."

May didn't speak. She was concentrating all of her small strength on getting the pack straps off her shoulders. She shrugged the left and then the right but the pack wouldn't go. She did it again, left then right, like the mule, but nothing moved. The pack stayed deeply burrowed in her spine. She stopped moving, then, and let her head push against the rock. She would have cried, if she'd had enough water in her body for tears. But she was dry, tearless.

She felt Anne's hands moving across her shoulders. For some reason, Anne was crying.

"Give it to me," Anne said, as she loosened by straps from behind and jerked the pack from May's back. The material of May's shirt went with it, soldered to the canvas. The skin of her back was exposed to the sun.

"Jesus," Anne said. She dropped the pack on the ground and knelt behind May. "Jesus. Your back is all blistered. I swear to God."

May felt Anne's fingertips running along the skin between her shoulder blades. She closed her eyes and let the cool fingers glaze her skin. She felt much better.

She stood up, turned and smiled. "Let's bury this shit, Anne." She bent over, her shirt front hanging like a bib over her breasts, and pulled Anne to her feet.

It took both of them to lift the pack from the ground and Anne's face grew red. "Has it really been this heavy all along?" she gasped.

"No. It's been growing all day, I swear." May looked closely at Anne's face. All her elegance was gone, her customary composure fled. "Maybe you shouldn't even touch it, Anne," she said. "Remember The *Lord of the Rings*? Frodo and Sam? Remember how, once you'd borne the ring, you could never be normal again? Remember how you couldn't even die normally, how you'd have to go to the Grey Havens and live some kind of weird half-life, forever and ever?"

Anne pushed her wet hair under her hat. "Yeah. And remember how Frodo couldn't do it, alone, and how even Gollum had a part to play? Don't quote to me, sweetie. I know the same stories." She smiled, a soft ghost of a grin. "You just want to get into the songs alone. You want to be the hero, 'Nine-Fingered May at the Canyon of Doom.' No way. I'm here. I get to play the faithful companion part, at least."

May laughed, right out loud. All her energy was coming back. "Nope, I've still got all ten fucking fingers here." She wriggled them. "So, okay. Heave."

They each took a strap and hoisted the pack into the niche. They each took one side of the flap and opened it.

But May alone lifted the Smucker's jar and found it, once again, almost weightless. She knelt easily.

It was very simple. She unscrewed the top while Anne dug a tiny trench with the tablespoon she'd brought along in the pack. She sprinkled the ashes, soft soft gray, no fire at all, into the trench and brushed the dirt back over. They each took a handful of sunflower seeds and poked them into the dirt, one at a time, in a circle around the hidden ash. Anne tipped the last cup of water from the canteen onto the circle, darkening the earth. They stood up and brushed their knees.

Anne scooped up the empty pack and slung it over her shoulder. She nudged May. "Say something."

"Oh Christ. What?"

"Anything."

"Well, okay. Dust to dust, ashes to ashes. Is that enough?"

"Perfect."

All of the others were on their mules, waiting, when they rejoined the group. No one mentioned May's shirt and the breeze on her back felt lovely as they ascended. It seemed fifteen degrees cooler for every ten feet up.

May noticed, at last, what she'd been told could happen deep in the canyon: you could look up and see the stars shining in the noon sky. You really could see them, little brilliant white lights in a sky as blue as heaven.

His last dream thought was very clear: "This has been a fatal mistake."

He woke in pain. He stayed in pain. All night. All day. He was trained to read and to read well. He understood the moral of this story. Just a few days before the dream, he'd seen May again after many months. Really seen her, touched her, held her, for the first time since just before the baby was born, and the feelings were still all there. All the old currents flowed. She was terribly happy and filled with hope, and the very next day she wrote him a letter.

114

Anne rubbed oil on May's back. The motel room was wonderfully cool. They'd turned the air conditioner up to ten. May sighed under the baptismal ease of the oil.

Anne's hands paused and she said, "Do you think everyone put ashes in there?"

May shrugged, nestling her face into the pillow. "Who knows? They shoved them under my door anonymously." She giggled. "Can't you just picture the whole English department tiptoeing to my door with their envelopes? In the dark? Way after hours? Jesus. What a thought."

Anne laughed and her hands ran again, gentle, swaying in circles. "Really. Who do you think did it? Lisa? Jennifer? Willie? John? Alex? Rose? Jamie?" She clicked them off her tongue, all their intelligent, sensible colleagues.

May turned her head away from Anne's eyes. "Who knows? I didn't count the envelopes and ashes all look alike. Probably not. Not Jennifer. She'd think it was way too weird. Not Alex. He isn't allowed to carry matches without his mother's permission." She giggled again, then paused. "Not John. Perfect wife, perfect baby. John has no sorrows, nothing to burn." She pushed her face into the pillow. "Keep rubbing."

Anne did. "I can just see it, though," she said. "From certain offices in the building, smoke rises. From certain wastebaskets, certain fake fireplaces, certain windows, smoke spirals. And people come, with their pathetic little offerings of ash. Bearing their dead. To you!" She smacked May's shoulder, very gently. "To you, you little damn saint."

May sighed, passing right on into sleep. "I do my best," she said.

New Hampshire Houses

NEW HAMPSHIRE HOUSES HAVE LONG MEMORIES. In this house, in this still-chill June of my thirty-sixth year, I lie awake at night and I think that if I stay very still, I will be able to hear the history I can't remember. Like the mice, it scrabbles and squeaks in the walls, making patterns of sound that fall just beyond the threshold of comprehension. Subliminal messages. It is important to search the sounds for sense, for signs. This history is supposed to teach me something, so I won't be condemned to repeat it.

So tonight I lie in a damp bed in a chilly room and I try to sleep. On the night table beside me is an old carved wooden box the caretaker found last month under a rotting floorboard in one of the sheds that connect the house to the barn. If you've seen New Hampshire houses, you know what I mean—the two-storey-plus-attic house proper, then a low line of sheds off the kitchen, running right into a high-ceilinged barn, so that in the bitter winters, New Hampshire people could get to their cows and chickens without fighting drifts. The sheds were also store-houses, full of the family's overflow from the house, repositories of all sorts of semi-precious objects.

Brownie, our longtime winter caretaker, left the box, with a note explaining where he'd found it, on the kitchen table— almost the first thing to meet my eyes when I arrived this morning. The box is locked and so it promises to be a treasure chest of sorts. I hope for old love letters, at least. It may belong to my family or it may not; I can't tell how old the box is. It was half-buried, dirty and stained, so it looks ancient, but it may not be. It could even be something as recent as a box of my brother's old comic books; it would have been like him to hide something just for the fun of finding it again, some future summer, and then to forget all about it. And then to die, leaving us to discover it.

Because there is so much potential in this box, I have decided to wait until tomorrow morning to open it. When the sun hits the huge granite rock my brother and I used to dive from, I will take the box down and sit in the sun and open it. Whatever is there, I will take as a sign. I need one, to tell me where my life should go next and so I have promised myself that this will be my lesson from history.

This house was built in 1842, so there was history here long before us, but I admit that it is only us, really, who interest me. My grandfather, my mother's father, bought the house, as a summer place, in the boom year of 1928. He was a master carpenter who built furniture and sets for the Zeigfeld Follies, during those glory years. After 1929, of course, Mr. Zeigfeld stopped paying his bills and my grandfather went broke. But he held onto the house; no one would buy it then anyway, way up here. No one had money and no one wanted it.

The early history of the house, before us, is in the wood

itself, in the planks of the floors and the beams of the attic. Ours is in the cupboards and drawers, in the things that fill the house, now. Most of these things are themselves old, musty and out of date. My mother never bought anything for the house, never even wanted to come up here with my father and my brother and me in the fifties and sixties, when we thought the place was heaven. She allowed my father, in his haphazard and bumbling way, to acquire modern appliances for the kitchen, but not much else was done to change the house in any way. The house always made her cold, she said; it never really got warm up here and the lake stayed glacial, chilling the air around it. My mother's bones always ached up here, she said, and she wouldn't come with us.

I've always thought that she just wanted to have our New Jersey house to herself for a few weeks each summer. That house was clean and spare and full of light; in that house, she could stay warm. I used to lie in this bed, all that time ago, and picture my mother at home, soaking in the hot backyard sun on the chaise lounge, with a pitcher of whiskey sours and a book, all by herself, happy. My mother never seemed to need us much. But I was happy too, in those days of freedom with my father and my brother. My father sat on the porch and read mystery after mystery, relaxing. Joe and I ran wild into the woods, up the hill and then down, into the lake. We would wade knee-deep in the blueberries, covered with mosquito bites and blue juice stains, unwashed and unbothered. Joe was seven years older than me, my instructor in wilderness behavior. My father and I came alone, in 1970, after Joe was killed in Vietnam. I was still only thirteen, that summer, but I felt much older. I decided I was a grown woman and didn't need to play and I picked the blueberries neatly into pails and used them to make muffins, to try to make my father smile. My mother, as always, stayed home. I imagined her there, in all that New Jersey heat, still unable to get warm.

I stop to figure it out. My mother was born in 1918 so she was fifty-two the year my brother died; my father, born a year earlier, was fifty-three. These seem like unimportant details, but I keep track of dates. They steady things and someday they will be all that anyone has to know us by—the dates on the headstones, the marriage and the birth certificates. No one came up, for a few years, after my father died in 1986. My excuse for not coming, summer after summer, was that I was busy finishing graduate school; my reason was that I couldn't bear to be alone with the ghosts. When I asked my mother to come with me, once, she laughed and said, "Never. I will never spend another night in that horrid old house." That was in 1987; my mother was sixty-nine and not likely to change her ways. One of her beliefs was in the superiority of the new over the old. She threw away antiques and bought new. Before my brother and my father were cold in their graves, she gave their clothes to the Salvation Army. My mother is not one, she says, to brood over what cannot be fixed or to hang onto what is gone. My mother is steady in her ways and sure of them. I don't even know what my ways are, although I have some hope that I can discover them, in this house. My mother has willed the house to me; she has no use for it, she says.

I turn on my side, facing away from the box, and promise myself five minutes of sweet memories to sleep on— the summers of 1990 and 1991, after I'd married and my husband Allen and I came here together. Our wildness was different from staining shins in blueberry juice, but just as delicious. In memory, at least, it seems to me that we made love in every improbable spot the house and the rocks and the woods and the lake could offer. Even, I remember, in the semi-dark of the shed where the box lay hidden. I decide to go to sleep remembering that—the cool dusty planks beneath my shoulder blades, the thin sun-stripes coming through the gaps in the old walls, and Allen's face above me. If I can just stay there, in that moment, I can forget that Allen and I didn't come back in 1992 and that now, in 1993, I am here alone, not any more resigned to the ghosts, just that desperate. But desperation is no pillow to sleep on and so I push myself back even further, and set the course of my dreams on the summer of 1965, when Joe was fifteen and I was eight and no one I loved had ever died.

The next morning is lovely, what my father always called a New Hampshire Chamber of Commerce classic—cool, breezy, the sky bluer than a baby's eyes. When I get up and stand on the porch in my nightgown, I can see and hear that the lake is full of energy, white-capped, pounding up along the rocks. It will be a good day to open the box.

I save up for that moment all morning. "It is June 10, 1993," I say aloud to the old walls, so that they will record this, too. "It is June 10, 1993, and on this day, in this, the thirty-sixth year of her utterly uneventful and predictable life, Annie Rosen will receive a sign and by that sign she will know if she should stay married to her husband, Allen Rosen, and bear his children." And the walls seem to ask, "Or? Or what? What else might Annie Rosen do? How else might the history of her life run?"

I shrug. "Or" is exactly the problem, isn't it? What history records is never the "or" or even the possibility that there ever was an "or." It only tells us what people did. It cannot begin to cover the agony of their choices or the lost potential of the alternatives. But what else is there, to guide us?

By 11 o'clock, the sun is on the rock. I put on jeans and a heavy sweatshirt and I take the box in my hands and carry it down the old path that runs through the blueberry bushes and the hemlocks to the boulders that line the lake bed. The box feels greasy and cold in my hands; it is stained by its years in the dirt—even dirt protected from rain and snow by the shed must have been full of dampness and the heaving of many frosts. The wood has patches of gray and patches of green on its sides and bottom; only on the top can I see the carvings of birds and flowers. The wood looks like walnut and it is heavy enough to be. I set the box on the sparkling granite; the lake is alive around me. The box is bigger than most jewelry boxes and is shaped like a shoebox, with a tiny old brass padlock, like a toy, on one side. I examine the box closely and decide that it was once a kind of lady's catchall box, her one small piece of privacy within her family's life. The box could hold her letters, dried nosegays, and locks of her babies' hair, braided with her own. If she was careful with the key, everything in the box would be safe.

I have picked up a loose chunk of granite along the path and now I raise it in my hand. I bring the rock down against the little lock and it breaks away easily, separating from the rotting wood of the box as if it had been longing for just this amount of force to help it let go.

It may seem impossible that, in all that fresh breeze, I smell rot before the box is even open, but I do. The air from the box is full of putrefaction and I know before I open it that this is a very bad sign. This will frighten you, I think, my hand resting on the loose lid. It's already frightening you. You will not be able to forget this and your life will change. Throw it into the lake, I think, now. If you open this box, you will know more than you wanted to know, know too much. But of course no one is that strong,

121

or that free from curiosity—if we were, we would not have history. I look off over the lake, now so brilliant with sun that my eyes dazzle. I am shivering in all of this sunshine. My mother is right—the lake is glacial.

I lift the lid and see, first, the little brass key, on top of a small bit of dirty cloth. The smell rises for a minute and chokes me, but it is almost instantly gone, carried off on the wind. I touch the little key with one finger; it is very cool. She did not ever intend to open this box again, I think. Whoever closed this box, closed it forever. She put the key inside and then she closed the lid and clicked the padlock shut. That, I think, is a desperate act. To lock part of your history away where even you yourself cannot ever draw it out again and touch it—this is a very bad sign and it is not yet too late to put the box into the lake, but I know that I can't.

Besides, somehow I already know what I will find in the box. It is not really a shock when I find the bones, very small bones. The bones are wrapped in old cloth, once white, now gray and green with damp. They are tiny bones and for a minute I let myself think that they are the remains of a cat or a puppy. But the skull is there, solid and factual, a skull I can cup in one palm, round and perfect.

I cannot hold that skull any other way than I would have held the child it belonged to. I bend my arms at the elbows and hold the whole damp bundle against my chest, the tiny skull nestled against my breast. There in the sun and the wind, I think that I can feel it dry out, become brittle and clean and I sit like that for a long time, rocking and letting the air do its good work.

My legs are cramped and the wind is cool. Before I settle the bones back in the box, carefully, I look for a note, a locket, some document, some sort of identification, but there is nothing. Whoever buried this child meant to leave no record. I get to my feet, stiff, cradling the box in my arms. I carry it back to the screened porch and leave it there on the old picnic table. I cannot bring it back into the house with me, now that I know what it contains. If I did, I would imagine that the smell that seemed to blow to away on the wind had come back, filling all the rooms of the house.

I fix hot tea to warm me before I go to the phone. I am dialing my own number when my hand stops and I realize that I don't want to talk to Allen about this. He will not, no matter how hard he tries, be able to understand the anguish of the woman who buried that box, alone, I'm certain. He will not be able to picture her, as I can, on her knees in that cold shed, digging. If she really wanted to get rid of it, he'd say, why not just put it in the lake, weighted with stones? But the lake is very deep and very very cold and she could not put a child in it, no more than I could. He will not understand why, but he will offer to come up here and comfort me or bring me home and I will have to turn him down, again.

I drink my tea, sitting by the old black phone. Finally, I dial my mother's number. Even she, disdainer of the past, cannot help but be interested in this relic.

She answers on the first ring, impatient as ever at seventy-five. "Yes?"

"Ma? It's Annie."

Her voice becomes wary. "Where are you? This sounds like long distance."

She can always tell. "I'm at the lake, Ma."

She laughs. "Cold as a whole coven of witches' tits, I bet. Isn't it?"

"No, it's nice. Listen, Ma, Brownie found something. I

want to ask you about it."

"No, wait. I don't care what Brownie found in that old dump. Why are you up there so early anyway? Where's Allen?"

"He's at home, Ma. Now listen to me."

"Home? Ha. What's wrong?"

"Nothing. Well, not much. I just wanted to be alone, okay? But I found this box...."

"Alone? You're up there all alone?"

"Ma, just shut up, okay?" I can actually hear her shutting up, as the sound of her lips closing over her teeth carries distinctly on the line. I wait.

"Okay," she says.

I take a breath. I can hear her really listening now. My mother's attention is enough to keep telephone lines taut, all the way to New Jersey. "Brownie found a wooden box, Ma. Under the floor of the first shed." I wait for her hoot of derision. I wait for her to say, "A box? Who cares about some old box?" But there is a long long silence. I can feel my muscles tightening and I begin to shiver. "Ma?" I say.

"Did you open that box?" Her voice has gone absolutely flat, all its sharpness honed away.

My knees feel shaky, even sitting down. "Yeah. It's a...."

"I know what it is, Anne. Don't tell me. Do not tell me."

I realize that I am almost doubled over in the old kitchen chair. I have drawn my knees to my chest and I am whispering into the phone. "Oh, God. Who's is it?"

She sounds like she is spitting. "You damn fool. You goddamn fool. Why did you open it? It was locked for a reason. Why didn't you let it be? Let it be, Annie. Put it back in the ground. Put it in the lake. Do you hear me? Forget it."

I try to catch my breath and I try not to cry. My mother

will not put up with crying. "Forget it? It's a baby, Ma. It's not an old newspaper. It's a baby."

There is a long time of just breathing on the line, first quick and angry, then slowing. "I'm coming up," my mother says. "Don't you touch it again." She pauses, then says, "It'll take me just a few minutes to get ready and then I'll be there. Ten-hour drive—I'll be there before midnight. Don't touch it. Let it be."

My mother has never, in my memory, come up here. But she's coming now and a kind of childish relief pounds into my chest. My mother is coming to be with me. All I can think of to say is "Can you drive all that way by yourself, Ma? Do you need directions?"

She almost laughs, almost sounds like herself. "Jesus Christ, Annie. As if I could forget the way. I'll be there before midnight. Do not touch that box again, hear me?"

"Yes, Ma," I say. "Drive carefully."

I spend the whole golden sunlit afternoon inside, away from the porch. I dust and sweep and I build a fire in the parlor fireplace so that at least one room will be warm when she gets here. I take all the glasses out of the kitchen cupboards and rinse them, throwing out the ones with cracks. I reorganize the pots and pans, stacking them by size and shape. I warm and air some old linen sheets by the fire and then make up the bed in the room my father always slept in upstairs. I don't know if it's the room my mother would prefer but it's the prettiest. It faces the lake and its wallpaper still has some color—the yellow roses running up and down the green trellises are still recognizable. I eat cold cereal for supper and then I just sit, wrapped in a quilt, and watch the fire. The quilt has been in the house as long as I remember. It's a unique pattern, one I've never seen anywhere else—spinning triangles of yellow and white and red on a dark blue ground. My brother used to say that the triangles were sails and he kept the quilt on his bed. After he died, I moved the quilt to my bed. Two years ago, Allen and I made love under it. I stroke the old stitches and I wonder who made the quilt. It's just always been here, part of the house, wrapped in its own history, absorbing ours. I try to picture her, the woman who created these sails of color. I wonder if the child in the box was hers, but I think not. The sails are so cheerful, so brave—I can't picture that same woman wrapping her dead baby in a piece of plain, unadorned sheeting.

As usual, my mother was right; she is here before midnight. I see the headlights coming through the pines on the driveway and I run to meet her. She lets the screen door bang and she hugs me hard. Her arms are like wires around my back. She is thin and stringy with age but otherwise not much different than I remember her in my childhood—bright blue eyes, a snapping voice, quick movements. The only time I can remember my mother moving slowly was in the days following the telegram in 1970, the ten days when we waited for my brother's body to come home. During those days, she was paralyzed. When it arrived, by plane and by train, she became brisk again and she moved quickly, to get him in the ground and at rest. My mother's name is Grace and I had never thought it suited her. Now I am not so sure.

"I'm stiff as boot leather," she says, stamping her feet and rolling her shoulders. "I only stopped once. And I'm hungry, Anne. Heat me some soup, will you? And make a whole pot of coffee. Use that old blue percolator that's on the top of the cupboard and make it strong." She holds out a tin. "I brought coffee," she says and then she goes toward the bathroom. It's clear she knows the way.

The percolator is white-speckled blue enamel and it makes coffee like thick syrup. Allen and I tried it once and went back to instant. I take it down, dust it off, scoop the coffee in, and set it to perc. The smell rises in the house like new energy and I see why my mother wanted it. I heat some chicken noodle soup in the least dented saucepan.

I find my mother in the parlor, rubbing her hands in front of the fire. "Damn icebox of a house," she says. "Can you bring my supper in here?"

I use one of the big round trays that have always leaned between the refrigerator and the wall. I arrange mugs and bowls and some bread on the tray and carry it to my mother.

She has pulled two wooden rockers up to the fire and put the coffee table between them. She nods. "Let's eat." She holds up a hand and adds, "No talking. No questions. Just eat. I'll talk later."

So we eat in silence and when my mother sets down her spoon and cradles her mug of coffee in her hands, leaning back, I take the tray away. I come back and sit down, facing the fire, sideways to my mother. I look into the flames. I've kept a good strong fire burning all day; I'm proud of it. "It can wait until morning, Ma," I say. "If you're tired."

"Jesus Christ," she says. "I drove ten goddamn hours to get here and you're going to hear this story tonight, so we can forget it. Tonight, Annie. Let's get it done."

I smile at the fire. My mother has been saying "Let's get it done" for as long as I remember. "Okay," I say. "I'm listening." I am listening, with all my heart. Whatever the sign is, whatever this story means, I've decided it's best to know, now. "Let's get it done," I say.

"All right, then. And listen quietly. Don't interrupt. Don't ask questions. I'm only saying this once." She cups her hands tight around her mug and she leans forward, hugging the warmth of the fire.

This is how I will always remember it: my mother, seventy-five years old and whip-thin, staring into the fire and drawing out memories more than sixty years old. I can feel the walls listening. Not only listening but recreating the story in the rooms around us, spinning it out from their long memories. Most of it happened right here in these rooms and the walls have kept their peace a long time. Now I feel them breathing the story out so that I will always remember it not as words spoken by my mother but as a kind of semi-transparent play acted on these floorboards and backdropped by these walls. I see this story happen and while it does, there is no difference between past and present: my mother is Grace Vose, seventy-five years old, talking; and she is also Grace Aylmer, fourteen years old, living this sad sad story.

It began for Grace here in this house in June of 1932, that dark depression year. Of course it began for her mother Lois long before that but Grace only knew that somehow, somehow, her mother had persuaded her father to leave them alone, to drop them off at the house and to leave them there in peace.

Grace was delighted. Her father had always been a casually cruel man who enjoyed teasing her, making her reveal her fear of him and then mocking her for being afraid. His cruelty became less casual, more calculated, after the 1929 crash, after he lost his work and his income. Mostly, it was Lois who suffered, putting herself between Grace and her father, but then Grace suffered from guilt.

That first glorious day of freedom, here in the house, Grace asked Lois, as they both rocked on the porch, how she had been able to convince him to leave them alone. Lois laughed. "Because he believes that I am carrying his precious son, that's how. The son he says he's waited twenty years for, putting up with a sickly, weak, near-barren wife."

Grace kept rocking, the sun on the lake flashing into her eyes. She remembered all the afternoons this past year when her father, sitting home with nothing to do, had led her mother off to their bedroom. Her mother's shoulders had looked small and tight as she followed him. Lois was forty-two years old that year and not strong; her lips were often bluish and she sometimes kept one hand pressed against her chest. But once, when Lois held back, planting her feet in the hall, her husband had simply looked back past her, into the living room and nodded at Grace. "If you won't, another will," he said, and Lois never held back again. Grace shook the memory from her eyes like stinging soap and kept rocking, but she reached over and took her mother's hand, and they rocked together, in the same rhythm.

That summer of 1932 became Grace's heaven. She climbed the hill and picked the berries and read books on the porch and turned brown from lying on the rocks in the sun. Her mother was slow-moving, quiet and patient. She grew heavier and heavier; she spent her days rocking on the porch, her evenings rocking by the fire. Grace was quick and strong; she was her mother's caretaker, her cook and her entertainment. But the months moved forward and September came before Grace could stop it. She was afraid she would be sent home, to school, but her mother said no, not this year. This year, for now, she was needed here.

Their only visitor that summer was an old woman from the village named Mrs. Hanson. She came by twice a week with groceries, fresh eggs, butter, milk and fruit. Mrs. Hanson worried Grace. She had a high laugh and shining eyes and, on every visit, she took Lois into the bedroom, the sunny front room with the yellow rose paper, and closed the door. Once, in mid-September, Mrs. Hanson left the door ajar and Grace crouched in the dark hall, peering into the sunlit room through the crack. She looked in and then she was sorry. She had not wanted to see her mother, heavy on the bed, her skirts pulled to her waist and her knees spread. She had not wanted to see Mrs. Hanson's gray head pressed against her mother's huge bare belly and Mrs. Hanson's hand between her mother's legs. But Grace was frozen there and she heard Mrs. Hanson laugh and say, "He still thinks it's not until Thanksgiving, does he?"

And Lois's voice, from the pillows. "Yes. He has promised, on the phone, that he will leave us alone until October 1st. Then he will come to get us, to see that his son is safely delivered in New Jersey. He says he'll come before any chance of frosty roads."

Mrs. Hanson drew her hand from between Lois's spread legs. Grace could see that her hand was wet, shiny. The shininess made her feel dizzy and she drew away from the doorway as Mrs. Hanson wiped her hand on a towel.

She laughed again. "By October 1st, his son—maybe—will be right here with us, honey. And maybe...." She leaned over and whispered in Lois's ear. Grace couldn't hear what she said, but she heard her mother's reply: "Oh no. No. I only wish for a girl. I want no sons. I will not give him a son."

That evening, in front of the fireplace, Grace sat on the floor and leaned her head back against her mother's belly as her mother sat in her chair. They had taken to sitting inside all the time now, as the days were cold. The leaves were already dropping from the tall maples and chill breezes made their way into the house from all angles. Grace wrapped her mother in sweaters and quilts, to keep her warm, and she fed her soup and sweet, thick cocoa. Her mother was easily chilled, her lips and fingertips blue.

Grace could feel the child's movements under her head, a constant restless rolling. Her mother's belly was enormously wide; the rest of her body seemed to have shrunk, absorbed into that teeming belly. Sometimes, Grace imagined that she could hear the baby singing. She knew it was just the sounds of the passing blood and the beating heart but, to her, there was music beneath all that, just discernible, just below the threshold of understanding, a distinct melody and rhythm. Her mother, too, hummed softly to herself, as she stroked Grace's hair. They spoke little; there was no need.

After she had seen her mother safely to bed, Grace rolled herself into the sailboat quilt Mrs. Hanson had given them and she rocked herself, in the small back bedroom. Before she slept, she slipped her fingers between her own legs and brought them back out, wet. She held the fingers to the moonlight and they, too, shone. Her body was like her mother's. She was content, and slept.

But late in the night, her mother called and brought Grace out of deep sleep. She ran to her mother's room and found her standing in a puddle of liquid, liquid with a strange ripe smell, not urine, as she had at first thought. Her mother was holding on to the bedpost and moaning softly. As Grace watched, she saw her mother's great belly, straining her nightgown, rise into a hard pulling mound, stay unbearably taut, and then, slowly, subside. Her mother cried out and took Grace's hand. Grace led her back to the bed and helped her to lean back on the pillows. Lois said, "Call Mrs. Hanson. Tell her it's time. It's early, but it's time. Go."

Grace ran. The telephone was a new installation in the house but she knew how to use it. She picked up the heavy black receiver and asked the operator for Mrs. Hanson. She was alert and calm when she answered, a woman used to being wakened after midnight and told, "It's time."

Grace sat by her mother and waited. Mrs. Hanson came quickly and she sent Grace downstairs. "No, child," she said, one hand on Lois's pulse and the other on her belly. "This is not for you. Wait downstairs. Stir up the fire and wait. This will not be long. She's ready."

Grace did as she was told. She waited by the fire, wrapped in her quilt. When she could stand it no longer, she crept up the stairs and knelt by her mother's door, resting her cheek on the hard old oak. She listened. She could hear a confusion of sounds: groans, cries, and instructions from Mrs. Hanson. Finally, a thin high wail and then, another. Then long silence.

She sat there, tears running, until Mrs. Hanson pulled the door open and saw her. She was holding a wooden box in one arm. She smiled. "You have a sister, Grace, a tiny little sister. Go see her."

Grace went to the bed. Her mother was asleep already, her closed eyes sunk in patches of deep gray. Beside her, wrapped in white, lay a tiny wrinkled baby with bright red hair, the color of her own. She touched the baby's curled fist and then answered Mrs. Hanson's call to come away and let her mama sleep.

In the kitchen, Mrs. Hanson was putting on her coat. The box was on the kitchen table. Mrs. Hanson gestured at it. "That needs burying, Grace," she said.

Grace stared at the box.

"It happens sometimes." Mrs. Hanson's face looked blank, tired, but her eyes frightened Grace and she shivered, her feet bare on the cold linoleum floor, her nightgown wrapped around her shins.

"It was a twin," Mrs. Hanson said. "Too small to live.

Never breathed." She stared at Grace, hard. "Now listen, girlie. Don't you dare upset your mama over this. Don't make a fuss. Your mama doesn't even know about this one—she fainted away after she saw that little girl. And she was smiling. Don't you ruin your mama's joy." She put her hand on Grace's shoulder. "This is best anyway; your mama hasn't got the strength to feed and care for twins. This is best." She turned to go and then looked back, her hand on the door. "You're a full-grown woman, nearly. It's your job to protect your mama. Bury that box or throw it in the lake. It don't matter. Just keep quiet about it, hear me?"

Grace nodded and the door slammed shut, leaving her alone with the box and her duty to her mother.

Grace shouldn't have looked but she did. She unwrapped the little cloth bundle in the box and looked. The baby was tiny, but no smaller than the one upstairs. Its hair was just as red. She touched its tiny fist and ran her hands over its perfect little legs. Its skin was blue but no bluer than her mother's lips.

She did the best she could, alone. She wrapped the baby back up, put the little key from the lock on top of the wrapping and closed the box. She snapped the padlock shut. She couldn't put the box in the lake—it was too cold and too dark and too full of unknown creatures. She lifted a loose board in the first shed and she dug a deep hole in the soft sandy dirt below it. She lowered the box into the hole and covered it with dirt and replaced the board, nailing it down tight. The sun was already up and shining by the time she put down her tools and wiped her hands on her nightgown and said the closest thing she knew to a prayer: "Dear God, please accept my baby brother. Thank you."

Grace hasn't looked away from the fire once. She just stops talking and the players fade from the room. That little-girl Grace, with her knees all stained from kneeling in the shed, is gone, and this Grace, old and wiry, is back. We sit in a kind of ringing silence, filled with echoes and shades.

Finally, my mother looks over and says, "But Annie, I heard two babies cry that night. I heard two cries. And I've never told a soul, until now. I heard two babies cry."

I nod. "Yes, Ma." She is shaking and I go to her chair and wrap the quilt around her, the sails decorating her shoulders. She touches my hand.

"And what you did was right, Ma. Not telling, I mean." I kind of hoist her up and lead her toward the stairs. She weighs almost nothing; I can lift her like a child.

"Was it, Annie?" she says. "Was it right?"

My mother has never asked me before, ever, if she was right. She just always is. I nod again and take her up, one stair at a time. "It was the only thing you could do. That little red-haired baby girl was Aunt Eva, right? And you raised her, right, after your mother died in 1940, long after your father had left? You brought her up, all alone."

At the top of the stairs, my mother nods. "I did," she says.

I try to lead her toward the front bedroom, to the bed I've made up clean, but she won't go in.

"No. I want my old room," she says and she turns into the small bedroom where I've been sleeping for years. "I'll be better here." She closes the door behind her but then opens it again. "You know, Annie," she says, more like herself, "you're a good listener. I appreciate that."

"Goodnight, Ma," I say and I take the front room and all night I listen to the history that runs behind the roses, wrapping around the trellises, and I try to make it make sense. There is only one thing that I am sure of—my grandfather did not deserve a son. Just as he did not deserve his daughters.

My mother is perfectly all right at breakfast. She finishes off four pancakes and two cups of coffee before she refers to last night's story. Then she just nods toward the porch. "It's out there?" she asks.

I nod. "In an old carved box. It must have been lovely once. Walnut, I think, covered with little birds and flowers, morning glories, twining all around the sides."

She snorts. "I remember it, Annie. The box belonged to the house; it was here when we bought it. Sat right out there." She points to the mantel in the parlor. "We kept odds and ends in it—matches, pencils, maps, and whatnot." She sips at her coffee. "I guess Mrs. Hanson took it up with her that night. I found the things from the box dumped in my mother's wastebasket. I never said a word."

I look out the kitchen window, into the trees. The pines are sifting down a fine golden-green pollen that coats the ground. Even the granite rocks are gilded with it and they shine. When I was a child, I thought that the June pollen fall was magical, a sprinkling of fairy dust. My brother, I remember, was allergic to it; he wheezed and coughed his way through every June. "Do you think that means she planned it, Ma? Mrs. Hanson? To have the box ready and all?"

My mother sets her cup down. "I don't know. She was just ready for anything, I guess." My mother shakes her head and runs her hand through her hair. "Damn old witch. She was prepared, that's all." She stands and takes her dishes to the sink and then leans over, looking out. She turns and looks at me. "You planted begonias in the window box here?"

I nod. "Yes. Pink and white. Pretty, aren't they?" I stand up. "I'll do the dishes, Ma. You sit."

She takes the dishes from my hands and puts them in the sink. She holds my elbow and points at the window box. "That's what my mother planted in 1932—begonias. The only year anyone was here to water them all summer. They bloomed like crazy. Bright red." She shakes my elbow. "So you're staying here, all summer, to water those? No sensible woman plants flowers she won't be able to take care of."

I look out the window. "I don't know. I'm thinking about staying."

She pushes me back into my chair and stands above me, her hands on my shoulders. "Annie," she says, "what's your problem, at home?"

"Oh, Ma. It's just life, you know?" I look up at her.

She nods and sits down in her chair. "So what's wrong with life?"

It sounds stupid to say it. So commonplace, really, in this house of long dark history. "It's Allen. He wants a baby. I'm not sure. We haven't been getting along that well lately and I'm just not sure."

My mother doesn't say a word.

"He almost had an affair," I say. I look at her and she still doesn't say a word. "I don't think I can trust him anymore, Ma. I don't know."

"He almost had an affair?" Her eyes are big. "What the hell does that mean?"

"Oh, you know. He was about to and then he told me. He was so sad about it. He felt funny, he said. He didn't feel right, with this other woman. But we didn't feel right anymore, either. You know?"

My mother is laughing. Her head is down on the table on her folded arms and her shoulders are shaking.

"Ma," I say. "This is not funny, Ma."

She raises her head, tears on her cheeks. "No, of course not." She wipes her palms across her face.

"Really, Ma. Things are lousy."

She looks out the window. "So they are, sweetie." She stands up, swinging an arm toward the porch. "But, still, we have bones to bury. Let's get it done."

We do the dishes in our old places. She washes and I dry and she tells me what she's decided to do, now, with her brother's bones. This time, she says, she has me here to help her and it is daylight—she will be bolder and do a better job. This time, the bones will stay buried.

She drives us up a dirt road I have never been on. I am holding the box on my lap. A shovel is on the back seat. The day is soft and gray, cloud-covered and warm. The road comes out next to an old wooden church; its windows are boarded up. The church stands in an overgrown field. Daisies and wild blue lupines have mixed with the grass to create a sea of foamy blue and white and green around our knees as we carry the box to the small cluster of headstones behind the church.

My mother carries the shovel and she knows exactly where she's going. There is a grave on one side, under a big oak, and she points at its stone—Muriel Hanson, 1864-1934. Beloved Wife and Mother. She smiles. "She didn't last long, after she murdered your uncle, did she?"

I stand holding the box in my arms. My uncle. This tiny baby boy, who never lived a day, my uncle? What could that possibly mean? "How did you know where she was buried, Ma?" I ask. "I thought you never came back, after 1932."

She stands, looking down at the stone. "I came back," she says. "The summer of 1970, I came up by myself. And I looked her up, that summer, and found her here." She nods at the stone, as if she and Mrs. Hanson had had a long visit that year and worked things out, between them.

"You came in 1970? After Joe died?"

She nods again. "I stayed that whole week, after his funeral. Don't you remember I was gone?"

I try to remember, to think back to that summer. I was only thirteen but it has always seemed crystal clear to me, that summer when the circle, the charm that held us all together, safe, broke. But I don't remember that my mother came here and now it occurs to me that the circle was broken long, long before. I just never knew it. My mother did. "I don't remember that, Ma," I say. My arms have been straining around the box and I feel the muscles getting tired.

"No," she says. "Maybe you wouldn't. I told everyone I was staying with Eva, anyway. But I wanted to be alone and so I came here." She shakes her head. "Froze the whole damn week." She turns around and holds out her arms, the shovel dangling from her left hand. "Give me that. You dig this time. You're younger."

I have a hard time letting go, but I slide the box into her arms and take the shovel. "Where?" I say.

"Right at her feet," my mother says, pointing down at Mrs. Hanson. "Let them lie together." She laughs. "Maybe they'll have something to talk about, my baby brother and Mrs. Hanson, on the long cold nights out here."

While I'm digging in the sandy dirt at Mrs. Hanson's feet, my mother is sitting on the ground, leaning on the tree, humming to herself. The box is on her lap and her fingers are tracing the design. She says, "Boys are hard to love, Annie. And men harder yet. They die in wars, they go away for no good reason, they are always stubborn and sometimes mean. Good ones, like your father and your brother and Allen, they break your heart almost as much as bad ones, like my father. Revenge is easy, Annie." She strokes the box. "But loving them is hard."

I look over at her. I'm sweating and I'm breathless and I'm trying to make sense of what she's trying to tell me.

She smiles. "My mother had a brother, too. His name was Preston and he died in France in 1918. My only brother died here in New Hampshire, in 1932." She rocks the box. "Your only brother died in Vietnam in 1970." She looks out over the swaying lupines and then at me, leaning on the shovel. "And if you think it's hard to lose a brother, you should try burying a son. You're right to be scared, Annie. I shouldn't have laughed. You're absolutely right."

I nod. I bend and dig. I stop when the hole is maybe two feet deep. "Ready," I say.

She gets up and carries the box over. She looks down and says. "That's not deep enough, Annie. Christ. I dug a deeper hole, at night, by myself, in the cold and the dark. It wasn't my fault the goddamn frosts heaved it up." She glares at me.

I put the shovel down. "It's deep enough for these few tiny bones, Ma. I'm taking the box back. Give it here."

She holds on to it. "You're taking him out?" she says.

"Yes. I'm taking him out and then I'm taking the box back. It belongs to the house. It's not ours, Ma." I hold out my arms and she slides the box to me.

I kneel on the ground and open the box. I slip the little key into my pocket and then I lift him out. His bones are already as light as air. I cup his skull in my hand and I gather the cloths around him and I lower him into the hole. My mother puts in the first shovelful of dirt and I fill in the rest. We replace the sod on the tiny grave together, on our hands and knees, as if we're praying. We sit back on our heels when it's done and we wipe our hands on our shorts and we smile at each other. We stand up, brush off our knees and go back to the car.

"Will you stay a few days?" I ask her, as she drives back to the house.

She shakes her head. "Not on your life. I'm going home, where it's warm."

I nod, not mentioning that she's sweating now, in the humid air. "I think I'll stay awhile yet. I want to sand and polish up the box." I touch its carvings. "It will be beautiful when I get the stains out."

My mother looks at the box. "As I recall," she says, "it always was a little stained. It never was perfect, Annie."

"I know, Ma," I say. But I look at the fine walnut and I think that it can still be nearly perfect if I sand and rub and oil, hard enough.

At Home with the Candidate's Mistress

T HERE HE IS, THERE HE IS, THERE HE IS. THE bastard. Look at him," Julie says, her finger right up against the TV screen. "Just look at the bastard."

She doesn't need to point. I can see him perfectly, even on my tiny black and white TV, its picture grainy and segmented by the wavy horizontal lines that always seem to shimmy across the screen at the most dramatic moments in any show, just when Sam is proposing to Diane for the ninth time or when Jean-Luc Picard sits down, cocks a cool finger and says, "Engage," stress on the "en." But Julie is excitable and she's also a little bit drunk, so she keeps jabbing her finger at the screen. "Look at his fake smile, look at his hair, for Christ sake. It looks like paper mâché." Julie stops jabbing long enough to tip her wineglass all the way back, chugging the last swallow.

His hair does look funny: it's a solid mass instead of individual strands. Of course, I'm used to seeing his hair more relaxed, I guess is the way to put it, definitely informal. Damp from the shower, curling just a little behind the ears. Or flattened in back from the pressure of the pillow. Rumpled all over from the tracks of my fingers. Here, on TV, it does look strange, as tightly controlled as his smiling jaw muscles, as smooth as the pink linen skirt around his wife's hips. Yes, pink, I'm sure of it, even in black and white: baby girl pink, innocent and pure and wifely. "I see him," I say. I wish for a commercial to take him off my TV screen, out of my living room, out of my sight and, like magic, one comes.

Julie sits back beside me on the couch, still vaguely pointing. "Did you get a load of that dress on The Wife?" she says. "Adds thirty pounds to her butt, at least." She pats my knee. "She's dumpy, kid. Really. You're in much better shape. Want some more wine?" Julie stands up and reaches for my glass.

It's still full. "No thanks," I say. "I'm fine. Help yourself."

Julie takes the five steps required to get from my living room to my kitchenette. "Really, kiddo. You're a whole lot prettier, even if you are five years...." She stops, pours her wine and sips at it. "Got any chips?" she says, rummaging around in the one cupboard.

"Older," I say. And I am five years older than he is, probably eight or nine years older than his wife. I know that I'm not supposed to be, according to tradition. I should be about twenty-three, a lean-bodied fluffy-haired blonde, a would-be actress cum model cum file clerk. But I'm not and that's the truth. I'm thirty-eight and my hair is already half white, although I still keep it long—my Emmy Lou Harris look, he calls it, and begs me not to color it—and I do not work out and I have no visible muscles. I'm not an actress, unless you count the performance aspect of teaching five sections of composition at the community college.

Figure it out: 35 freshmen per section; that's 175 papers a week to grade. It keeps me busy in the evenings. I have a master's degree and I read a lot. That keeps me busy on holidays.

The TV flashes back to the convention but, for the moment, he's not visible. Now let's get this straight—my particular man is not *the* man or even the second or third in line. Mine is that guy about four rows back on the platform. Yes, he'll make a short speech. Sure, he's running for an office, but not *the* office. Don't let's get this mixed up with the big time. It's not. This is strictly small stuff; world peace does not hang on this man's shoulders. But some things do.

Julie comes back with a bag of Doritos and a full glass of wine. "So where's the slime hiding now?" she says, settling down on the couch, her legs folded up, Indian style, my sisters and I used to call it, when we were kids. She tears the bag with her teeth.

"Cut it out, Jules," I say. "He's not slime. He's just ambitious."

"Yeah. So was Macbeth, just ambitious, and things still got pretty bloody around the old castle, didn't they?"

Julie reads, too. She's my office mate at the college. She's been divorced, twice. Her kids are grown. Her apartment isn't much bigger than mine. "And, really," she says. "Did you see that dress? Like something your mother picks out and makes you wear to grandma's house or to church or something. Gross."

"As compared to my lovely outfit?" I say, leaning back to pose.

Julie looks over and laughs. "Well, hey. The gray sweat suit look is in, you know? Especially with the blue bandanna around the head, the circles under the eyes and the chewed nails. It's a kind of natural elegance."

"My nails are not chewed—they're just short from typing," I say. Typing, it's true. I have been typing, a long manuscript. Long because it's all there, the whole story, neat and in order and well-documented. Because I am not some brainless bimbo. I have collected, and kept, proof: letters, notes, hotel receipts, telephone machine tapes. He wasn't very careful, at least not at first. I was. After all, I'm trained in footnoting, proper citation of sources and use of only verifiable facts.

I haven't told anyone, not even Julie, that I have this, the complete record of this affair. I've certainly never told him. I don't know why I have it, exactly. I don't expect to use it, either for blackmail or for profit or for revenge. But sometimes, at the end of an evening, when the papers are all graded, when my eyes are too tired to read, I like to look at the evidence, just touch it. It's proof that it happened, that I didn't make it up, that he has, for three years, loved me. He has; he's said so. He's even written it down. He is that trusting, that sure I'd never betray him. He is that vulnerable.

"He's ba-ck," Julie says, using that intonation that I hate.

And he is, smiling, stepping to the podium to begin his speech. His wife, in pink, I'm sure of it, stands where the wives always stand, just to his left, just a pace behind. Her hair, too, is perfectly smooth and certainly tinted, blond. She keeps her hands folded in front of her, her arms pinned to her sides. I wonder if she's afraid of sweating, afraid her nervousness will come right through, right there on TV, ruining the expensive linen. She is, after all, only human. She knows about me, of course. In the beginning, when he was careless, and almost carefree, when he thought he really wanted a divorce, he told her all about us. She told him she was pregnant, which was true, and he wept. Things settled down, between them, and divorce was never mentioned again, nor was I. Now he's careful; he doesn't even call until two or three a.m., when everyone in the world, except me, is asleep.

Tonight, at home in their beautiful brick house behind the smooth green lawn and trimmed shrubbery, sitting with her nanny, is their daughter, two and a half years old, a natural blonde, all sweet and powdery in her cotton nightdress. At least that's what I imagine. I have never met her, never even seen her, except in the snapshots he shows me. But I know what she must smell like, that perfect clean, freshly bathed smell of a cherished and privileged daughter. I do know that smell, although I have no children of my own. I was a cherished child, once, and I sometimes think that I can remember the smell of my own childhood flesh.

"Blah, blah, blah," Julie says, as he speaks.

"Shh." I listen and I look, trying to catch the man I know in the black and white image on the set.

Julie settles back, crunching Doritos. She is a friend; she lets me watch in peace. It's not the words I care about. Those are standard: the party, the platform, the country, the people, the world, family, church, whatever. What I try to find is the man himself; I try to catch anything of the man I know in a gesture, a smile, anything real and human that slips through.

And there it is. Simple—his hand reaches up, for just a second, as if to loosen his collar and I see all the times he's arrived here, rushing, at 5:30 in the afternoon, pulling off his tie before he's over the threshold, unbuttoning his top button, throwing his jacket on this couch, laughing, relaxing, taking off the mask.

Julie snorts, loud, as the applause begins. I try to laugh with her, to be cynical, to be hard, as he reaches to his left and draws his wife into the circle of his arm. He kisses the top of her hair, carefully. I see that she is much shorter than I am; her head barely touches the shoulder of his blue suit. She waves to the applauding crowd and I see that I was right—her dress is wet with sweat. The lights must be hot and she is under such terrible scrutiny. She smiles and smiles and smiles, until it is over and someone more important takes the microphone.

Julie is making rude noises and I think that she is still snorting in disgust but when I look over at her, her cheeks are all wet. "The bastard," she says. "How can he do this to you?" She stares at me.

"Oh, Jules," I say, patting her arm, brushing the crumbs off her sleeve. "He can't help it. He just can't help it. Come on," I say, shaking her arm. "Don't you cry, for God's sake. Look at it this way—at least I don't have to dye my hair or put on that horrible dress and worry about my antiperspirant failing." I laugh. Really, I suddenly feel much better.

Julie shakes her head. "You're just being brave," she says. "And stupid. You are being really stupid, you know that?"

I know that. But I say, "Hey, listen, Jules. Think about this: all over this country tonight there are women like me, watching their candidates on TV. There are hundreds of us, in our little apartments, in our sweat suits. We are, think of it, legion. And we have the fate of the free world in our hands. We have the power to bring down empires. We have proof. We have evidence. We can ruin them all, bring them all tumbling down like blocks. We are in control." I jump up and stand on the coffee table, waving my arms, making the victory sign, Nixon-style. "We have the power, we have the power."

"Oh sure, you're tough." Julie laughs, then she points through my legs at the TV. "Oh my God. Look."

I turn around, still standing on the table. Way down there, tiny and no higher than my knees, is the black and white image and it shows me that I was wrong, earlier, in what I'd imagined. They didn't leave her home with the nanny. They brought her. Even though it's late and she must be sleepy, they dressed her up and bundled her out to the platform, first to stand between them and then to be lifted high on her daddy's shoulders, where she looks scared and clasps his head in her arms, holding on for dear life. Her mommy reaches up to steady her, a hand on her leg. They smile. All the candidates smile. All the candidates' families gather, smiling and waving. The little lines come back, dancing across the screen, and everything goes wavy.

I crouch down and turn off the TV. Without it, it's very quiet in the apartment.

Julie stands up and knocks on my head, very gently, with her fist. "Hey, in there, you with all the power. You gonna use it?"

I shake my head. "No."

Julie bends down and shakes my shoulders hard, not gently at all. "And you, you in control. You gonna answer that fucking phone when he calls later, three or four a.m., full of bullshit love? Are you?" She shakes again. "Are you?"

I look up at her and shake my head. "No. I'll try not to."

Really, I will. I'll just lie there, and I'll keep my arms folded across my chest, holding on for dear life, wishing for a mother to reach over and steady me.

A Midsummer Night's Dream
in Middleton

YOU ARE READY TO THINK THAT MARY AND
Michael Smith, Susan and Samuel Jones, Joan
and Joseph Brown are laughable, not real, not even
real characters but caricatures and not even good ones at
that, not broadly enough drawn, too unadorned with sa-
tirical flourishes, too—admit it—boring. After all, they
are all middle-aged, middle-class, middle-income, and they
live in nearly identical brick houses in Middleton, New
York, a town located just exactly halfway between New
York City and Albany on the banks of the Hudson which
at that point is, just as you'd expect, a middle-sized river
which never floods. The founding fathers of Middleton
were so unimaginative— and probably the founding mothers, too—that they couldn't even give their little town a
factually interesting name, like their near neighbors in Salt
Point, a place where, history shows, herds of cattle being
driven down from the farm regions upstate to market in
the city were stopped and allowed to lick freely at salt blocks,
something which cattle apparently love to do, their mobile,

almost prehensile, tongues wrapping luxuriously around the roughly textured squares, so that when the herd was stopped again, shortly before New York, for water, they would drink and drink and drink (the same strategy is employed by bars, of course, who serve free salty snacks), thereby increasing their salable weight by maybe ten fluid pounds and the farmers' profits by some few dollars, not even counting the considerably valuable satisfaction of having outfoxed the city slickers.

No, the founders of Middleton probably just glanced at a map, noted where they were, relatively, and left it at that. Still, it's grown to be a pretty little town, with its square green lawns, its trees ripe with time, and its rambling roses grown to the roofs of the brick houses. Absolutely indistinguishable in most respects, as you might expect, from the hundreds of towns in New York, and probably the nation, named Middleburg, Middletown, Middlebury, and so on. (Although Middlesex raises some interesting thoughts, doesn't it?)

But Mary, Joan and Susan, Mike, Joseph and Sam are individuals, each made of unique flesh, molded by all the forces and accidents in the universe which somehow (somehow—it is such a mystery, think of it) deposit certain strands of DNA in certain patterns that create certain composites of blood and bone and brain and which then align those particular, singular creatures not only in the same era and nation but on the same street in the same neighborhood, in three adjacent houses attached by three adjoining back yards where their children tossed balls together as babies, where backyard barbecue smoke scented their common air, where prom pictures were snapped and weddings consecrated, where even now grandchildren play together, in proof of another cycle. Listen to me: these people are not ciphers, not bland or blank or flat. They are as real and full of feeling as you and me and, like you and me, they ache for more of life than they've been given and their reach, at times, exceeds their highest grasp. They are the heroes of their own story and so let's get to it: coming in right here, as Susan serves coffee to Joan and Mary in her kitchen on June 22, 1996, and reiterates her plans for their mutual celebration of midsummer in the ancient, sacred style of the Celts she's been studying, a celebration held outdoors, around huge and blazing fires that will light the quiet Middleton sky with strange orange incandescence and where anyone may freely fuck anyone else and all resulting births, although this is an unlikely eventuality with all participants over fifty, will be considered, as they must be, children of the Goddess, with medical expenses shared by all.

Mary stirs heavy cream and Sweet'n Lo into her coffee. She's aware that this is an incongruous combination but it really tastes wonderful and she already weighs over two hundred pounds and is rising, so so what? "Aren't open fires illegal inside town limits?" she asks.

Susan opens the oven door to check her oatmeal cakes; she is cooking Celtic foods these days, although authentic recipes are hard to locate. She's willing to compromise. "Only if you burn trash, I think."

Joan is drinking her black coffee iced. Her collar bones show through her chest flesh and she jiggles in her chair, full of caffeinated energy; she wears a sleeveless shirt, something the other women gave up ten years ago, acknowledging the downfall of their upper arms. But Joan's upper arms are smaller around than Mary's wrists and they are burnt brown from the sun the other women also abjure. Joan is not afraid of cancer; she has it already, deep in her liver, where she's kept it hidden, so far, from family and friends. "Oh, let them arrest us," she says. "Imagine, hauled off to jail naked, our faces painted blue." She laughs into her glass, making steam rise from her breath on the ice.

Mary shifts her weight on the narrow kitchen chair. "Do we have to be naked?" She looks down at her very large breasts which rest on the table top like loaves rising, outwardly still but mobile within.

Susan shuts the oven door gently and puts her towel over her shoulder. "I don't think they're ready yet," she says. Her once-red hair is now short, sensible gray but her eyes are still scandalously green, full of catlike lights. "Not completely naked," she says amiably. "We can wear deerskin cloaks."

"Oh fine," Joan says. "I'll pick one up at the mall." Her laughter turns to icy mist, again.

Susan sits down and picks up her mug, a rough cream-colored ceramic splashed about with her grandchildren's overlapping handprints in different-colored paints. Her daughter-in-law is a potter. "Well, we can really wear whatever. It doesn't matter. What matters is the spirit. We just need to cast off our modern shackles and remember the matriarchs, the priestesses. We need to celebrate the summer solstice in the old way, under the open sky, free to assert our own sexuality." She stops. She doesn't have to convince her friends. They are converts already, although it had taken some time to make Mary understand exactly what the solstice is and that it's not connected somehow to the federal government and daylight saving's time. Susan rises and gets the flat cakes out of the oven. They are a bit heavy, hard to bite into, with an uncomfortably gritty texture, but with plenty of butter and jam, they're edible. Even Joan downs half of one, before she has to run.

They've already agreed to meet, with their husbands of course, to play the roles of King Stags, in Susan and Sam's back yard, which is the middle plot, on Midsummer night's eve. So there isn't that much to discuss.

And before you mock them too much, these suburban celebrants, you might tell me what you know of the solstice and what we need to do, to properly celebrate its coming so predictably, so faithfully, in every year of all time since time as we know it began and really long before that, because the solstice, as you may, being wiser than Mary, know, has nothing to do with how we count time, with our calendars or our clocks or the Greenwich mean. It has, in fact, nothing whatsoever to do with us at all, and perhaps that's why, most of all, we need to bow before it, in primal awe. Or at least we need to fuck whomever we first stumble across, by the light of backyard fires, if that's the best we can do. Because human beings are so packed with hubris that we always do imagine that planetary motions, trepidation of the spheres, have something to do with us, don't we? We can't even think about such grand inhuman schemes without weaseling ourselves into the picture. Check your dictionary, if you want evidence. My dictionary defines solstice as "one of the two points on the ecliptic at which its distance from the celestial equator is greatest and which is reached by the sun each year about June 22 or December 22." See? Webster slides in our names of our months to make this incomprehensible grandeur seem homey. But the skies don't care that we've sliced our year into twelfths and named one of those twelfths "June" and another "December," do they? Of course not; the skies are oblivious. Ah, but what lovely words we have for the unimaginable, don't we? "Celestial equator"—a phrase that simply spins on the fulcrum of heaven and earth, measurement and infinity, all balanced by the mind of humanity. And what else should we do about it all? Well, history does indicate that celebratory sex is a tradition, perhaps our closest link to all those forces which beat in the blood and which we will never ever understand, so why not?

You'll have guessed, of course, that Joseph, Sam and Mike, separately and individually, were pretty easily convinced that free love under the balanced planets was a fine idea, that access to a wife other than one's own, in the service of spiritual renewal, was not serious sin. Susan's Sam was used to her strange schemes anyway; Mary's Mike was, to be honest, just a bit weary of fighting his way through all that flesh to reach the center of things, so to speak, and had lately dreamt of an easier target; Joan's Joseph was halfway aware of something amiss in his wife's chemistry, nothing he could put his finger on, just a slightly bitter scent to her skin, perhaps, and he wanted, sincerely, to have her back, safe, and prayer is prayer, after all.

Of course you will suspect, because even if you are too young to remember Peyton Place you will have watched the soaps, that at some time in their long lives as neighbors and friends, these three couples went in for a little swapping, a hint of swinging. Maybe in the sixties, when the barbecue mingled with sweet marijuana, or the eighties, when the white wine flowed? In between the babies and the grandchildren, in all those long summer afternoons, didn't even one husband leave work early and find his way, so simple a mistake, into the wrong house? Didn't he slip in the side door, climb to the wrong bedroom, and slip his penis into a half-strange woman, familiar in all but her most secret movements and sighs? Didn't even one wife (you will suspect Susan, because of those catlike eyes, but there is no proof, no proof at all) leave her babies soft asleep in their cribs one spring morning and step through the fence, surprising her neighbor in his garage workshop and didn't they, for just one short breathless moment, sink down into the sawdust and hammer away together, in perfect time?

I say no: this never happened. The women loved each other too much to cause each other pain; the men, too, were honorable friends. Oh, of course they looked; they certainly imagined, from time to time, the taste of different lips but, no, never did they swing. Yes, but they are getting old now and they know it. They've lived through more than fifty summer solstices each (and fifty winter ones, too) and they've hardly had time to notice. But now? Now, well, they feel it all slipping away and sometimes the time is right, or at least, necessary.

Besides, Susan, with her green green eyes, has convinced them that at Beltane — or Midsummer or June 22 or whatever we puny humans choose to name this particular note in the music of the spheres — no man is Sam or Mike or Joseph and no woman is Susan or Mary or Joan; all are priestesses or stags and all, all serve the Goddess. On Midsummer eve, Susan says, they will shed their familiar skins and don the cloak of divinity. But even as the earth itself is made of matter, stone and soil and sea, so are they made of solid flesh and it is in their flesh they celebrate.

So, at 10 p.m., Eastern Daylight Saving's Time, as they count time in Middleton, on June 23 by the kitchen calendars, and in the year one thousand nine-hundred and ninety-six by the admittedly flawed accounting of solar years since the birth of one particular god, Susan and Sam, Joan and Joseph, and Mary and Mike met under the open sky. The moon, that night, was in her first crescent, thin and sharp. (A verifiable fact: check your almanac, if you must, for June 23, 1996. And tell me, quick, upon which hand a waxing moon rides — your right or your left? You can't call up this sight you've seen a hundred times, or more? No, I will not tell you. Go look at your sky.)

They were not naked but had all wrapped themselves in some sort of dark robe. In the dark, no one would know a J.C. Penney's bathrobe from a hand-tanned deerskin anyway, without an acute sense of smell and smell, that ancient aphrodisiac, is somewhat dulled in modern humans.

Susan lit the fire, carefully prepared on a square of bricks in the center of her back yard. It wasn't, to be sure, as large a fire as she would have liked but she wanted no interference from the volunteer fire department or curious neighborhood children. No, it was really a small tidy fire but even that had its effect. Try it sometime, on a night in what we call June, when the fireflies themselves are alight and pulsing in your back yard: light just a small fire and see how your eyes are drawn into it, how flames in the night usurp familiarity, how its draft draws strangeness in. Try it: use sweet-smelling apple wood, an old charm for fertility, if you dare, and take the time to breathe very deeply. You should, if you haven't lost all of your native senses, be able almost to taste the roses on the roof, the honeysuckle on the fence, the hanging bracts of the old locust trees, the mulberries, the grass, the very dirt itself. Then maybe you will understand what happened on Midsummer's eve in Middleton. I don't pretend to, not really, so I'll stop here. Just watch. It's beginning.

The six figures circle the fire, holding hands as directed, going faster and faster and faster, running, rushing their bare feet through the cool slippery grass. Running, around and around, until they're dizzy, disoriented. Their hands break apart and they separate, still spinning.

Each woman, quite alone and quite uncertain of where she is, backs away from the fire, but keeps her eyes upon it. All of her sight is dazzled by the flames; the rest of the world is in deepest shadow. Each backs into a separate spot and there sinks to the ground, spreading her wrap under her bare hips. She meets the earth beneath her; it is hard and moist. She can feel the tips of grass on the backs of her thighs, like sharp teasing tongues. She can, as she throws her head back, see up, up through the branches of the maples, up to the stars in whose power she lies back and waits. Her nipples harden in the air and she opens her legs to the night breeze, which softens her. She stares at the sky and waits.

Each man, as he has promised, looks nowhere but at the fire; he is blinded by it and truly cannot tell who has gone where. He counts off five hundred pulse beats: it takes patience, especially as he feels himself already erect under his robe. When his wait is over, he walks away from the fire and begins to circle the perimeter of the yard. Each, quickly, finds what he needs: a naked woman, already open and ready for his flesh. It is all, for the first time in his life, so easy, so perfectly easy. No on has asked for love, no one has ordered him to put a rubber sheath over his most sensitive skin, no one stops for so much as a thought.

Each couple fucks in simple, earnest harmony and from three separate points in the yard, their cries arise, carried away by the smoke.

Oh, come on, you say. It didn't happen like that at all. Every one of them was guessing, a mile a minute. They were all aware of who they'd gotten: Michael, for instance, would certainly recognize the bulk of Mary or the bones of Joan or Susan's coarse clipped hair. They'd know, you say. It wasn't sacred, it was just seamy middle-aged sex, dressed up.

I don't know. Susan and Mary and Joan never discussed it afterwards; certainly the men didn't. And their thoughts, as ever, are their own. I'm not privy to anyone's thoughts. I'll tell you what I guess, though, if that makes any difference. I think that Susan had Sam, Mary Mike, and Joan

Joseph. That whatever accidents flung them together in those pairs in their blooming twenties did it again in their fading fifties. They loved each other. Besides, isn't that what the fairies out that night would do, the best of all possible tricks? Ah, but behind the fairies work forces that even fairies don't understand. So I believe that on that enchanted night, they were all young, so young that Mary's extra flesh just fell away and she became slim and supple; Susan's hair grew long and soft and waved in red curls over her shoulders. Joan was whole and well and strong and the men — well, the men were what young men are, in all their first fury and sweetness. I believe that on that night, they all found their same old mates but found them transfigured, found them gods.

Of course, you know that I can't know this, not really, but it is what I want you to believe. I want you to, so that you will try, oh please try, to trust in whatever the planets and the Fates and the fairies have in store for *you*, under the open sky.

The Last Case of Polio
in New Jersey

I WAS THINKING ABOUT PLAGUES THE OTHER DAY AND that reminded me of Bud and Dot Johnson. Bud and Dot Johnson were the golden couple of the middle 1950s, at least as we perceived couples then, in Ramsey, New Jersey: both blond, both tan, both young and in love, married right after high school graduation and immediately presented with a cozy little starter home by Dot's rich father, and soon thereafter presented with three blond babies, easy as pie. They were perfect; they shone. They really did. So of course they were doomed. Anyone can see that, in retrospect. Now that we've read our Bibles, our Shakespeare, our Aristotle, our Sophocles, we can see that if drama was ever to happen on our street it would have to strike there. The fall is only tragic if it happens to those above us, those both blessed and tainted, those whom we have always watched, waiting.

I, at least, watched Bud and Dot Johnson, diagonally, from my house across the street from theirs. So, yes, my vision of them is bound to be askew, I know that. Their light always struck my eye at an angle, from a point somewhere just beside my normal focus. And even then, I'm pretty sure, I realized that it was I who was offstage, peering intently from a darkened wing, and they who were front center, moving always in the glare of the lights. But did they know it, I wonder? Did they see themselves as heroes? Did they feel in their young bones the tiny hairline fracture of their particular flaw, that little crack which would soon gape wide and inspire in us fear and pity and, yes, exultation? I doubt it. How could they? Heroes were sparse in New Jersey, and Bud and Dot, I'm almost certain, had never read Sophocles.

I was reading *The Man in the Iron Mask* that summer and empathizing with the young prince encased in that implacable metal headgear more than I probably should have because I had a cast on my right leg. So we were both held, against our natures, the prince and I. Okay, so my prison enclosed just one leg, just an ankle really, broken by nothing more deadly than a misdirected swing of a neighbor's croquet mallet, and his prison was absolute, constructed of treachery and malice as well as cold metal, but there was still a sympathetic connection. It was easy enough then for me, a mere girl, to identify my trifling troubles with the glorious hazards and heroics of male literary adventures: that's all there was, remember? That summer I was especially vulnerable to imaginary connections anyway; I was twelve and couldn't run or ride my bike. For once, I was pretty much homebound. My mother set up two lawn chairs for me in the shade of our front yard oaks and she brought me cool drinks. I sat, ankle propped, and read and watched the Johnson children play.

The Johnsons' yard was across the street and to my left. Directly across the street there was nothing to watch. A Mr. and Mrs. Snyder lived there alone and quiet, almost sequestered. Neighborhood whispers were that Mr. Snyder was a war victim, shell shocked into unnatural passivity, a quiet, quivering man who spoke to no one. His wife gave us nervous little nods; they had no children for me to play with. It occurs to me, just now, that maybe the Snyders had a drama, too, a story of their own. I can suddenly imagine it. They were a young couple married, in an excess of hope and despair, just before the war, and then, just like that, an old couple, shattered into permanent silence. I can picture her at some train station, in her 1945-style suit, her Betty Grable hair, waiting, then watching him get off the train, blank in the eyes and not at all certain who she was. I can see them lose their youth, not gradually, but all at once. Maybe it went something like that, their story, and maybe it was worth knowing. But to my eyes, that summer, the Snyders were invisible. The Johnsons took up all of the available light.

From across the street, the three Johnson babies were almost indistinguishable in their perfection. Healthy golden-haired toddlers playing in the sun look much alike. Dot, still so young—what? twenty-one, maybe—still with her cheerleader figure and her shining blond hair, watched over the babies; Bud came home for lunch every day. He worked now for Dot's father's construction business, so he'd kept his football muscles, his lifeguard tan. He would wave to me, propped in my chairs; he'd been in my brother's high school class and they'd been friends. My brother was away in the navy. I was flattered that Bud still bothered to wave and I always waited for the lift of his arm. I loved to watch him move.

At the moment of Bud's arrival home for lunch, the whole family was like a tableau arranged for my eyes. The babies ran to their young father and hugged his legs; he lifted them in his arms, all three at once, a giggling batch of sunny flesh. He kissed his beautiful wife and they all went into the house together, leaving echoes of light behind.

Then, one day, an ambulance came for Bud and the children disappeared. It was early in the morning on an already hot August day. I called for my mother from my chairs and when she didn't answer I hobbled into the house on my crutches, yelling. "Mom. Mom. There's an ambulance at the Johnsons'. Its lights are flashing."

She ran from the kitchen, her hands foamy with soapsuds. She was wiping them on her apron. We stood together on our front porch, watching two men struggle to lift a stretcher with Bud Johnson's weight on it into the ambulance. Bud was smiling at them, joking I think, but not moving. When he saw us watching, he waved. I leaned up against my mother, taking my weight off my cast. "What's wrong with him?" I asked.

My mother shook her head. "I don't know." She took off her apron and handed it to me. "I'd better go ask Dot if she needs someone to take the children. You stay here." She walked across the yard, fast.

"Wait. I can walk, Mom. I'll come with you."

My mother turned and pointed to the chairs. "You will not. Sit down and don't you move."

I did as I was told. My mother wasn't gone long. She came back pale and sat on one of my chairs, next to my feet, her arms hanging loose. "What's happening?" I said. "Where are the kids?"

My mother looked up. "The kids? Oh, Dot's mother took them, late last night. When they began to suspect what Bud had."

"What does he have?" What, I thought, could be so bad they took away your children, late in the night?

"They're not sure," my mother said, picking up her apron from the grass and rising to tie it around her waist. She spoke quietly, not looking up. "But he can't move his legs. It looks like polio." She reached over and handed me my crutches. "Come inside, Margaret," she said. "Don't sit here staring." She waited for me to gather my book and glass and to fit my crutches into my armpits and then she held the door open for me, as I hopped over the threshold.

Polio. That word still shocked then. Polio. Maybe it still does, for those who remember it. Maybe that's one of the things that will always divide us — those who remember polio and those who don't. I don't really remember the sweeping plague my parents still sometimes called "infantile paralysis"; what I remember is its moment of extinction. I remember lining up outside the school health office in 1955 with all the other fifth graders in Ramsey, New Jersey, offering our bare arms to the syringes filled with the newly tamed virus. I remember the sting of the salvific needle.

The rest of the story drifted into my eyes and ears in bits and pieces. My mother picked up parts from the neighborhood women; I heard parts from the other kids. My brother sent parts home from the navy, even. But none of us knew, not really. So it was left to us to imagine the tragedy, to put it together from offstage, to experience it at a safe remove. Even so, it changed everything. Really, it did. Years later, my college roommates told me that whenever I got drunk, I had an annoying habit of wanting to discuss the book of Job. I always wanted to argue over Why the Good Suffer, and so on, ad nauseum. And that's true; I did. But what my roommates didn't know was how I pictured Job: for me, Job wears Bud Johnson's face. And so do Othello and Oedipus and even, sometimes, Lear.

But if Bud is to join their company, as we've learned, he

needs a flaw, and what was Bud's flaw? Was he so pious that he annoyed the devil? Was he proud and quick to anger? Ambitious? Jealous and susceptible to bad council? Maybe. We never really got to find out. Remember, he was only twenty-two when he caught polio.

The only thing even close to a flaw in Bud that I ever heard of was that he was afraid of needles. Yes, that's all. But it meant that he hadn't had the polio shot that came available that year. He declined to participate in, to take advantage of, the one genuine miracle of our time. He sent Dot and his babies, but he wouldn't go himself. He was so strong—why should he fear? So, was it hubris, plain and simple, after all?

Maybe—but, what did Dot do to deserve her fate? Or those babies golden in the sun? Why do the good suffer?

What I couldn't actually see of this particular drama, which was most of it, I imagined, lying in my bed at night, looking at the ceiling. I pretended I was Bud Johnson in his iron lung at the hospital. I thought I could imagine that, if I enlarged my cast to cover my whole body, if I forced myself to feel the totality of that enclosure, if I allowed myself to feel the iron sides pressing on my ribs, forcing the air out of my passive lungs, then quickly expanding, creating the vacuum that sucked air back in. If I could stand the knowledge of being worked upon like an accordion, I would understand. Some nights, I achieved it, I think. I was not breathing; I was being pumped. I learned, too, to lie absolutely still. I stilled my body, by will. Sometimes, late, I woke up rigid, unable to loosen into normal sleep. Truly, if temporarily, paralyzed.

Or, I imagined being Dot, brave and smiling, heroic. I'd bring Bud flowers and read him stories, feed him songs and soup and laughter and make him well, in heart, anyway. I'd save him. I'd love him so much that he would not curse God and die, would not even want to. These visions brought tears to my eyes, they were so lovely.

There were so many roles for heroes in the Johnson story. I could even imagine being one of those children — curly haired and angelic, like that little girl in *Silas Marner*, bringing hope and joy and generosity and light back into the darkened family, bringing smiles to my Daddy's face. The possibilities went on forever, forever intriguing.

For that summer, at least. In the fall, my cast came off and my pale itchy leg grew new skin. School started and I was in sixth grade, a year of great changes, a year when my closest friends began to get periods and to let us all know by publicly displaying the nickels they'd brought for the girls room Modess machine. A year when I pretended I'd gotten periods, too, for fear of being left behind in that sudden ripening that somehow promised to give us stories of our own, key roles in romances to come.

I stopped imagining life in the iron lung. The simple truth was, I was moving and Bud was not. And Bud's story had no suspense anymore. After the drama of the morning ambulance trip, it slowed down so. News came infrequently; the little green house stayed very quiet. The children pretty much lived with their grandmother. Yes, Bud came home, on a hospital bed that was rolled into the garage and somehow, from there, invisible to watchers, maneuvered into the house. He didn't wave, although word was that he could have, by then, because he'd regained motion in his arms and neck and shoulders. It was the rest of his body that resisted mobility: his chest and legs, hips and belly, and all the rest of, for me, unimaginable places, the ones that my mother whispered about to my aunts, saying mostly, "Poor Dot. She's so young; it will be difficult for her."

After Bud disappeared into his house and even after the children came back home, there wasn't much to see. At first, the Johnsons' lawn got ragged and long, but then Dot's brothers came to cut it and, later, Dot's brothers raked and burned the leaves. Dot's father's trucks plowed the driveway that winter and Dot's mother's car was nearly always there, parked out front, and so we knew that she was in there, helping. Dot's father put up the Christmas lights and took them down again. Dot's mother took the children to Easter services, dressed perfectly, in three matching outfits. Things were being managed, it was clear.

So the story seemed over, arrested somehow, before it ever got going. But I saw the ending, too, the following summer, by accident. I was up early, on a clear June morning, one of the first days of vacation. I'd been awakened by cramps, by the first real period I'd ever had. I was already bound by the belt and the pad my mother had handed me almost a year ago, in anticipation of this day.

I wanted, suddenly, to ride my bike, fast, away from the oaks of home. I was just about to start, poised in the shade at the edge of the yard, when I saw Dot open her front door and walk out. The children weren't with her; I knew, somehow, that they'd already gone to her mother's. Dot carried two heavy suitcases and she didn't look up. She was utterly exposed to me, there in the clear sharp air, alone in her sunny front yard. I noticed, without really wanting to, that she'd gotten fat, her ankles as wide as her knees. But what I saw most clearly was that her hair had turned brown. She walked to her car, put in her bags, and drove away.

I never saw Dot or Bud Johnson again. The retrospective stories that came back to our neighborhood were too simple and too sad to bear much repeating: he'd begun to drink, to rant, even to hit her as she bent over his bed with a tray. He'd become bitter, my mother said, and who could blame him, trapped like that, at twenty-two? But, of course Dot couldn't stay; luckily, she had her family. They'd always looked out for her, always would.

And Bud? I was at school when the ambulance came again, this time to take him to the nursing home, so I didn't see him go.

The house was sold to an ordinary family, with kids who didn't sparkle, who did nothing to attract tragedy, and so our street settled down, again, into the realms of the everyday. After all, by then, everyone had been vaccinated.

Sluts

I WANTED TO BE A SLUT. WE DIDN'T, I THINK, USE THAT
word, *slut*, in 1961 when I was thirteen but that is what
I wanted to be, from the moment I saw those marks on
Estelle Carter's breasts. The word for those marks, I knew
even then, is *hickeys* and it's a term as ugly as *slut* but it doesn't
matter because words can't touch the shock of admiration
I felt, and feel, when I think of Estelle Carter's sucked-on
breasts.

She was thirteen, too. Imagine: thirteen, eighth grade,
changing after gym, she just slid down her one-piece royal
blue bloomer suit with its tiny cap sleeves and puffed pants
and there, on breasts that actually needed the bra that
cupped them, were scattered pinkish-blue badges of experience. She didn't try to hide them; she just put on her
white cotton blouse and plaid skirt, kneesocks and black
flats and left for social studies.

Linda Reinhardt, at the locker to my right, flipped her
ponytail in disdain: "Estelle's a pig," she said. "She lets boys
feel her up." I know, today, that that's what she said but I

heard it then and pondered it for weeks as "She lets boys feed her up." I often confused words and sounds in those days. I think it was a kind of aphasia associated with adolescence. I swear that my blood so often filled my ears with its own tidal pounding that I could not hear correctly and so perceived a muffled combination of others' words and my own liquid urgencies. That image of feeding was more startling than feeling anyway, and more true to those hickeys. It involved Estelle and boys and mouths and breasts somehow in configurations that kept writhing around in my head. I tried to imagine all the possibilities but, in the end, none mattered. Only one concept remained certain—awe and admiration for the one girl I knew who was brave.

Oh, I know, I know. I've grown up now and I've learned the correct way to understand Estelle Carter's hickeys: Estelle Carter was a misused, unfortunate child, a typical product of a broken home. This, in fact, was true. Estelle's mother was divorced; Estelle and her wild brother (at sixteen he drove a motorcycle and quit school) and her mother lived in a tiny cement-block house near the edge of a wet woods at the very bottom of my road in the suburbs of northern New Jersey. Her mother waited tables at night so she never once sat in the yards on summer afternoons and drank lemonade with all the other neighborhood women who had husbands and who talked and laughed out loud in the soft light under the oaks on Oak Ridge Road and who went home in plenty of time to start supper, snapping their lawn chairs shut with sharp bright clicks. Mrs. Carter slept all afternoon and when we were much smaller, before Estelle became a slut, if I wanted to play with her I had to tiptoe around her house, being very quiet. My mother didn't like me playing with Estelle even then;

she was, she said, not at all sure about that brother, who even before he became a bona fide hood was still a worry, a slick-haired boy who smoked and threw stones with deadly accuracy, but who did not pitch for the local little league.

Moreover, I'm a woman now and I know that a thirteen-year-old's breasts are not fair territory in anybody's game. I know that Estelle Carter probably got pregnant at fifteen (my family moved away from Ramsey, New Jersey when I was fourteen, so I don't know this for sure) and had to quit school and lived a life thereafter even harder than her mother's. I know that female bravery is not best displayed by bodily recklessness. But I admire her still, because I am a grown woman and I do know that opening your shirt for a man and letting him suck does take courage. Yes: she lets boys feel her up and who's to say if one won't have a knife in his hand, or teeth like razors? The heart lies so close beneath the breast.

My oldest sister, in 1961, was twenty-four and unmarried, a bit of a problem in itself, and pregnant—an enormous problem. She lived at home and one-half of her paycheck as a file clerk in a law office went to my parents for her room and board. I think it's important to say that— she paid her way.

We younger girls were not told about this pregnancy; we only saw my mother's face grow tight and heard my father rage. I'm sure, although my hearing was odd, that I heard my father call Penny a pig, over and over and over again, on the night she must have broken the news.

The man, finally, was invited over to our house for a civilized discussion although my father had referred to him only as "that greaser" for years. His name was Tony Bianca and I liked him for the time he'd played pinochle with me when I was sick and the way he waved up at my bedroom window when he and Penny were leaving for a date. He never really turned around and looked up at me sitting in the dark behind the curtain but he must have known that I was there watching because he always tossed me a little backhand wave just before they climbed into his car. Penny looked beautiful on those dates; her waist was drawn in by a wide elastic belt and her breasts, in a pointy bra, were proud under her short-sleeved sweaters. I think I just loved my sister's young grown-upness. I know I loved to watch them go.

Whatever happened in that discussion that night was not exactly civilized, although of course we weren't told that either. Penny explained many years later, over the bottom of a bottle of wine, so I'm not absolutely certain of the accuracy of details: Tony Bianca left that night, shortly after asking my father how much he'd be paid to marry my sister. He never once came back, never once called, doesn't to this day know if he has a son or daughter. They'd dated for seven years.

So Tony Bianca didn't see his baby left behind in the vegetable garden, but I did. It happened, it seems now, in a series of whispers. First, my mother whispered to our officially gathered female family members, four daughters called together in the basement rec room as though things of this sort could only be spoken underground, that she would be having a coffee for the neighborhood ladies and at the coffee an important announcement would be made. I think of us there; collectively called the "girls": my mother, Penny, Linda, Rita, and me. My father was at work and my brother was in the Navy in Japan. He sent Penny, soon after, a musical jewelry box with a swaying geisha doll inside. I don't know what he knew. I think of us girls and we had only one striking characteristic, as a group—we all had some shade of red hair, varying from Rita's true copper to Penny's delicate rosy blonde to Linda's and my dark auburn. My mother's hair was just then turning gray.

My mother never looked at Penny, deathly pale at her side, and she never told us what the announcement would be. She said she had already sent out hand-lettered invitations, saying "Come hear our news! Coffee at Priscilla's. Tuesday, June 3, 11 a.m."

"They'll see," my mother said, "that I'm not afraid to face them with this. They'll see that I stand by my daughters, no matter what." And she began to plan the menu.

Coffees were the official variation on the theme of afternoons under the oaks except that coffees always took place in the morning, promptly at eleven. Good china was used and the housewife's baking was on public display in a series of cakes and cookies and pies. My mother was, and is, a superb baker and her coffees were popular. In fact, my mother was a versatile entertainer. During baseball season, the ladies gathered around our TV to watch afternoon games and drink pitchers of strong whiskey sours. Those afternoons sometimes became riotous and the returning husbands found no suppers on their tables when they got home. But coffees were sober affairs and this one hung like a portent around the house for a week.

But, despite what old wives say, the atmosphere didn't kill the yeast and the sweetened breads rose and the tarts were light and puffy. On the selected Tuesday, all of us girls were to stay home from school and dress up and go to the coffee. We'd never gone to one before; my oldest sister, of course, knew why we were being initiated at this one and the next two down may have had an inkling but no one told me. At thirteen, the youngest, I hadn't a clue, except the memory of the word *pig* and that was enough to link the planned coffee with both my sister and Estelle Carter and I knew it had something to do with courage.

But Monday came before Tuesday and changed everything. On Monday morning I was allowed to stay home from school to help prepare for the coffee and so I was there when the whole house smelled sweetly of baking and Penny, paler than ever, came to the kitchen. I heard this truly, I think, because I was right there, mixing the dough for the hermits, the cookies that no one but my family can get right because no matter how many times my mother gives out the recipe she never tells the other women to cook the raisins before stirring them into the dough, so they'll be soft and full of flavor.

"Mom," Penny said. She had a hand on the back of a pink kitchen chair; she swayed.

My mother turned, her eyes steamy from the stove. She was stirring fudge at its critical stage and couldn't look away for more than a second. She turned back to the bubbling pot.

"I'm bleeding," my sister said.

I stared at her. She wasn't bleeding, not that I could see. Her face looked whiter than the refrigerator but she wasn't bleeding. She was wearing a white sleeveless blouse and lemon yellow pedal pushers and there wasn't a sign of a wound on any part of her body.

But my mother believed her, I could tell by the back of her neck. Her hand stopped stirring the fudge and she lifted the spoon and watched the dark syrup drip into the cup of cold water she had set by the stove. If the drops held together in a firm ball, then the fudge was ready. She molded two drops between her thumb and forefinger. I

could see that they were still squashy, not ready. She put
the soft mass of mushy fudge into her mouth and began
stirring again. Her back stayed to my sister. "Go hoe the
peas," she said.

"What?" My sister's voice was a whisper and she really
was swaying. I'd like to say that I went and stood next to
her but I didn't. I kept blending soft warm raisins into
spicy hermit dough.

My mother spun, holding the wooden spoon coated with
wet chocolate in her hand like a wand. She was smiling.
"You heard me. Go hoe. Hoe hard. When that's done,
mow the lawn."

My sister's eyes were filled with fear. I could see that.

"Penelope," my mother said, although we always called
her Penny, "this is your way out. Go on."

And she did. It didn't take long. She never even had to
do the lawn. I watched my sister through the steamy
kitchen window. She moved like a demon along the rows
of peas in the backyard vegetable garden, swinging the hoe
above her head and slamming it into the earth. She
stretched and bent, stretched and bent, maybe a hundred
times before even I could see the wound. Then, the back
of her pedal pushers was soaked with blood, and finally,
the blood ran down her legs and stained her shoes.

My mother, who didn't drive, called the ambulance then.
She'd poured the fudge into greased pans and told me how
to cut it into perfect one-inch squares when it was properly
set. The hermits were in the oven and I knew when to take
them out. My mother washed her hands, picked up her
purse, and went outside to wait with Penny, who was allowed to sit down on the grass at the edge of the garden.
My mother put her arm around Penny's shoulders and

Penny rested her head, for a minute, on her shoulder.

The ambulance men took my sister from the garden and my mother went with them, but they were back from the hospital before supper, my mother saying that Penny had had a small hemorrhage, some kind of mishap with her periods, and she'd be fine. Penny was put to bed and when I looked into her room later that night, she was asleep on her side, sucking her thumb.

On Tuesday, we had the coffee. We were all dressed up and there, except Penny. My mother poured coffee with calm hands and told the concerned ladies that Penny had had a fainting spell. To them, she never said the word *hemorrhage*. I know, because I was listening for its dark sound. If any one of them was suspicious, she could never voice it. What were dirty suspicions in the face of perfect squares of fudge, cherry tarts with edges like a picket fence, and hermits no one could duplicate?

Of course they asked, though, what was the announcement? My mother's invitation had promised them an announcement, they said. Yes, come on, they insisted. Tell, tell.

I watched my mother's face. She smiled. "Well," she said, folding her hands in her lap. "Well, girls." Her nodding head included my sisters and me with the other ladies. "I'm expecting."

There was a moment of absolute stillness. My mother was forty-one years old that year; I, her youngest child, was thirteen.

Then they began to laugh and sigh and congratulate and giggle. They surrounded her like rushing water, their good summer skirts swaying softly around their hips.

That coffee was an enormous success. Afterwards, my

mother filled a plate for Penny and I carried it to her room. She sat up and ate it all, smiling like Christmas.

I sat on the edge of her bed, fearing blood. My sister smelled bloody. I'd had one period and I could recognize that smell, not quite hidden by pads or light summer blankets.

"So," she asked, "what did Mom tell the old hens?"

"She said she was expecting," I said.

My sister stopped chewing and stared at me. "Get out."

"No, really. She did." Did she think I'd get that simple word mixed up?

Penny sat very still and then she said, "That lying pig."

But it was true, or at least it came true. The following April, my little sister Sarah was born, ostensibly four weeks late. She was a large baby, close to nine pounds, with fiery orange fuzz for hair. My mother had been seventeen when Penny was born; she was forty-two for Sarah. Her years of fertility seemed like they'd go on forever, I imagine, but now she is seventy-two years old and frail, her bones brittle as winter twigs. All of her daughters have children of their own, even Penny, whose womb healed and strengthened, after that one small mishap and who met her future husband, a college-graduate accountant, not six months after that day in the garden.

Now Sarah is thirty and I doubt she knows the story of her genesis. We didn't talk about it and we were all so much older than Sarah; we all mothered her.

And I've thought and thought, as I climb my own forty-second year. How did my mother manage it? She must have gotten pregnant after she made her announcement. Just like that. As if it were easy. As if she could just open her blouse, and her legs, and it would happen as she wished, just one more act of courage.

And why? As if she owed the earth a living child.

One other thing—that day when I saw Estelle Carter's breasts, we'd been made to go outside in our gym suits to play kickball with the boys. I protested, saying to my gym teacher, "I don't want them to see me in this." This—the baggy blue bloomer suit so ugly it ached.

She looked back at me and glared. "If you don't like the way you look, you shouldn't look that way. Get outside."

As if, at thirteen, one could help the way one looked. Change it. Change anything.

As if I could become a shameless slut, like Estelle Carter, like my sister and my mother, at will.

Gypsies in the Place of Pain

WHEN THE GYPSIES CAME AND CAMPED IN THE hospital waiting room, anything seemed possible, for a while. Our little world of 9-South widened, for that week, and something of the strange and magical was let in. After they left, carrying their healed daughter away in their arms, I stood in the empty waiting room and just breathed their air. It still smelled different from ordinary hospital air—spicy and sweaty, smoky and free. I miss the gypsies. But that's the whole point, I guess: gypsies go and we stay.

The gypsies had come, as all the old stories warn us they will, suddenly. One minute the hospital halls were full of us ordinary parents and our ordinary sick or wounded children and the next they were full of slim, dark-eyed men in tight black pants and loose white shirts and lush, dark-eyed women in full skirts of many colors. The gypsies spoke fast and loud in a language no one else knew and its strange cadences silenced our usual hum of Spanish and English, as we all stopped to listen. In one afternoon, the gypsy women took over and transformed the parents' lounge, spreading bright blankets on the floor and over the vinyl couches and drawing out packages of food from their deep bags and bundles. The gypsy men leaned against the walls of the lounge, smoking dark cigarettes and eating from plates of food carried to them by the women.

Up and down the hall, ordinary parents drew their children, those who could walk or wheel about the corridors, in close. The old stories say that gypsies steal children, but when the gypsies had gone, no children from 9-South were missing and no changelings had appeared. Of course, our children were poor candidates for stealing—some would have died by nightfall without their IV's, their respirators, their transfusions. Our children were quite safe from gypsies. In fact, before she left, the gypsy grandmother made charms for many of the children, to protect them. My son Ted still has his, even yet, taped to his latest dressing—a small triangle of different-colored threads woven together with pieces of straw.

I wasn't exactly surprised when the gypsies arrived on our floor but I was still amazed. Delighted, actually, to see that gypsies really do exist, just as we've been told—a tribe, a people entirely foreign but here among us, after all. Not legends but flesh. I wasn't surprised because my son's surgeon had pulled me into the 9-South supply closet to tell me they were here, early on the day they came. He'd done a classic "Psst," crooked finger invitation, as I walked by the closet on my way to face a terrible cafeteria breakfast. It was pretty laughable, the great and handsome surgeon, huddled in the closet, sitting on a giant institutional-size box of Pampers, waving me in.

I went in and leaned against the shelves stacked with boxes of syringes and sterile tubing and tried to look perfectly normal. "Yes, Doctor?" I said.

"Close the door," he said.

"Wow. Is this a proposition, Alex?" I asked, wishing it were and knowing it wasn't.

"Just shut the door, okay?"

I reached over and swung it shut. "Damn. No lock," I said.

He put his head in his hands, half laughing, half moaning. "You won't believe this," he muttered. "This is too weird to believe."

He was wrong about that, of course. I believe anything. You can't spend years hanging around Babies Hospital in New York City and maintain a normal sense of incredulity. Really, as the bumper stickers say, "Shit happens," and unbelievable shit happens to our kids all the time. But I didn't want to answer him right away; I was just enjoying looking at him in close closet range. He is a golden man, blond and tan as only the rich and privileged seem to be. And he was wearing his surgical greens and white sneakers, my favorite outfit. He looked young and rumpled, as vulnerable as any guy caught in his pajamas.

Okay, so it's not hard to tell that I'm half in love with him—the classic mother-falls-for-her-kid's-doctor routine. But it's exactly that: half in love. I am emphatically not in love with Dr. Alexander Harvey, the chief pediatric surgeon who marshals his troops and marches them around the halls in the mornings, pointing at the kids in their rooms like they're cases in some ever-changing file cabinet and making little jokes to entertain the interns: "This is Ted, who got the worst of both worlds. Nature screwed him up and lousy early medical care made him worse." This is Ted, I think back at them, a polite smile on my face, my beloved, intelligent, funny, wounded, eight-year-old son: look in his eyes, you pompous bastards, and weep. But I am in love with Alex, who often shows up alone, at odd hours, looking weary, and who sits on the end of Ted's bed and trades sports stories. This Alex sends Ted tickets to Giants and West Point football games and this Alex once took Ted out of the hospital, removing all the tubes he would later have to replace himself, and transported him to Yankee Stadium, a few blocks away, by subway. So, sure, I'm half in love with my son's surgeon and why not? He loves my son, I know that, and he loves him because he cannot cure him, not because he can. Give the man credit: it's real easy for big-ego surgeons to feel fondness and gratitude, almost, for their successes and real, real hard for them to love the failures, the patched-up, cob-job kids we hold together with tape and spit and guts, walking reminders that medicine is not magic. On 9-South, we call these kids repeat offenders, and we laugh.

He lifted his head and looked up.

I smiled and sat down on a box, knee-to-knee with Alex. "Okay. So what is too weird to believe?"

"Gypsies," he said. "There is a whole pack of gypsies in my office downstairs."

I'll admit that was unexpected. "Gypsies? Like real gypsies? Gold hoop earrings, shawls, crystal balls?" I was harking back to my favorite Halloween version of gypsies, the costume we could always whip up at the last minute. "Gypsies? In New York?"

He nodded. "Not only that. The princess of the gypsies is lying on the couch in my office, right now, with a fever of 105. Lois is trying to find her an endowed bed."

Lois is Alex's secretary—a hero in any time and place. She lets me use her typewriter to type papers for my correspondence classes and she once let Ted sneak an X-ray of a Mickey Mouse toy, posed so that Mickey was giving everyone the finger, into a pile of films Dr. Harvey was presenting at a fancy medical conference. It was a big hit and now they keep it in the files all the time.

"They have no insurance, of course," he was saying.

"Wait: the princess of the gypsies?"

"Yeah. The honest-to-God princess of Romany, I swear—or one of them, anyway; she may not be first in line for the throne—is in my office." He rubbed his face with his hands. "She's six years old. She's pretty sick. And they brought her to me, because they asked, at other hospitals, for the best pediatric surgeon in town. So, of course, someone mentioned me." He said this with not a stitch of false modesty; one of the things I love about him is his absolute hubris. "Now they won't let anyone else touch her. I understand that her father waved a pretty big knife at an intern who tried to divert them to the emergency room, instead of my office." He grinned. "Her father carried her right into my office, put her into my arms and said, 'You will fix my daughter's kidney.'"

I laughed. "Or else?"

He nodded. "That was the implication. They have her films, from another hospital, and he's right about the diagnosis. She's got an obstruction and one kidney is a mess."

I looked over his head, at the piles of clean white sheets. "Can you save it?"

He touched my knee. "Sure. It's not as far gone as Ted's was. And her obstruction isn't bilateral and she doesn't have all the other complicating factors. Sure. It's really pretty simple; they're lucky they came here first, before somebody else screwed around with her. But she is a sick kid, right now." He stood up and stretched. "And I better fix her. I have a feeling that if I don't, my first-born son is a goner."

I tried to laugh. Alex's first-born son is named Chad. He's a chubby kid who comes in with his father on weekends sometimes and plays video games with Ted. He's a nice kid.

Alex tapped my head on his way out. "She's coming to this floor, the princess. And the whole gypsy encampment, I bet, will follow her. Keep watch."

I smiled. "Good. It will make a change around here. And I want my fortune told."

He left the door open and I sat back on the box, looking at the floor. I didn't want my fortune told, not really. What if we all had knives, I thought, and what if we all threatened to take their firstborn, if they couldn't save our own? What if it were that simple—one day we all just stopped smiling and being polite and keeping our lips stiff? What if we wailed and rent our breasts and demanded justice? It was worth thinking about.

Because when the gypsy parents came on the floor, that's what they did. Or at least they let their anger and their fear show as their little girl was put in the bed in the single room at the end of the hall. Her father wouldn't let the orderlies put her on a stretcher; he had carried her in his arms, her little dark head tight against his chest, all the way up in the elevator, the nurses told us later. The nurses had a very hard time getting near her to take her temp and start her IV, her father hovered so close. Her mother stood a little aside but her eyes were fierce and she watched them so closely that it made them nervous, the nurses said, and they had to stick her twice. They were sweating, they said, when they left the room and they drew straws to choose her night nurses. No one wanted to work under the pressure of the gypsy parents' eyes—royal gypsy parents, at that.

By that afternoon, the gypsies had taken over the lounge and the security men had been sent up, again and again, to explain that it was only for parents and to explain the rules about smoking and how many visitors the children could have at any one time, and so on. There was a lot of shouting and then I guess a compromise of sorts: her parents could sleep on cots in her room, as we all did, and her grandparents and a few other close relatives could stay in the lounge. The few others amounted to about twenty-five people and they all roamed our hall in bands of bright color and strange talk. They stuck their heads right into our rooms, pointing at our children and waving their hands toward our TV's and video games. They observed none of the usual dictates of hospital etiquette, the rules of proper parental behavior that say, basically, "Don't stare at other people's pain."

An old woman dressed all in black, the princess's grandmother, it turned out, came all the way into our room. I was reading and Ted was sitting up playing with his guys—small action figures he keeps spread across his bed table, arranged into elaborate warring factions. His big stuffed cat, a round black scowling thing that he loves, sat at the foot of his bed. At night, sometimes, Ted tells me stories he's made up about this cat, whose name is Fuzzle. He leans down from his high bed over my cot and says, "Hey, Mom. Want to hear an exploit of Fuzzle?" And he goes on to tell one, some outrageously wicked adventure of Fuzzle, a cat with no scruples whatsoever: bad-tempered, foul-mouthed, vengeful and gleefully mean. They're a riot, those stories.

The woman came right in and touched the cat. She looked at me and said, in oddly accented English, "For luck?"

I nodded. "For luck."

She shook her head and touched Ted's foot under the sheet. "Is there luck, in this place?" She waved her hand, to indicate the whole hospital.

Ted looked up at her and grinned. "Sure," he said. "Bad luck."

She nodded and tapped his foot. "This is a smart boy," she said. She looked over at me. "A smart, strong boy." She turned and left our room. Behind her she left a scent. It smelled to me like cloves, a warm dry smell. Comforting.

I felt sudden tears on my cheeks and I walked to the window, to keep them from Ted. I looked out into the late graying afternoon. There is a small rocky park just across Broadway from the hospital; its few trees were bare. I'd almost forgotten that it was November, nearing Thanksgiving. In here, time is all the same. The temperature in the halls remains steady, summer and winter. The windows don't open.

I looked into the street, where normal everyday people were walking home from work under the low sky. In the park, bunches of other people were gathering; I could only see a funny, foreshortened view of them from up here on the ninth floor, but I realized who they were—gypsies, hundreds of them. They had come from somewhere, from everywhere, to camp outside the hospital in the cold. I felt a little hiccup of hope in my chest: if gypsies still existed and if they came like this, rising out of the streets of New York like mist, when and where they were needed, wasn't anything possible? Anything at all?

For days, the gypsies stayed in the little park and they actually had real campfires. Ted and I sat on the wide windowsill in the evenings and looked down on the spots of orange flame nine stories below. Ted began to make up a whole new series of Fuzzle exploits—Fuzzle and The Gypsies. In these adventures, Fuzzle learns a lot from the gypsies about knives and horses and crossing palms with silver. As I recall, Fuzzle also teaches the gypsies a thing or two, about pure unadulterated meanness and spite.

While the fires burned outside, the princess was feeling

better inside, the antibiotics working on her infection. She got out of bed and walked the halls with her parents or her grandmother and she smiled shyly at the other kids. She was a pretty little girl, all eyes and shining teeth and black curls. Someone, I think it was Nicole, the four-year-old with leukemia, showed her how to ride on her IV pole, standing on its base while her parents rolled it down the hall. Someone else, probably Richy Nicovic, who'd just awakened from a two-year coma and was anxious for action, showed her how to ride the IV pole all by herself, handling it like a scooter, pushing one foot along the floor for acceleration and then lifting both feet onto the base and just sailing. The nurses smiled at her as she cruised along, her IV bags rustling in the wind her passage created. They're good like that here. They let the kids be kids, whenever they're able.

I noticed that Dr. Alexander Harvey stayed off the floor most of the time, because as soon as he showed his face, he was surrounded by gypsies, waving their hands and asking questions, looking at him with burning eyes. Even the supply closet wasn't safe any more because the gypsies had become used to going there for their supplies, as we all did. Some parents hinted that the gypsies were stealing boxes of diapers and stacks of sheets, but I never saw them take anything but what they needed, day to day, like anyone else. We all make our kids' beds ourselves and most of us even change their bloody dressings. I've gotten real good with the complicated sterile dressings on Ted's central line; I wear the whole get-up—gown and mask and gloves—and I've got the procedure down. That line goes into the vena cava, just above his heart, and it feeds him. If I want to take him home someday soon, I have to know how to take care of that line. If you've got a kid that can't eat enough to keep himself from starving, on his own, you learn. All of us learn.

I bet that if the gypsies had had to, they'd have learned too.

But Alex did come up one night, late, and he sat down on the end of my cot. I was half asleep and I just curled my feet up, to make room for Alex. It was nice—cozy and homey, in a way—to have him sitting there.

Ted, who was supposed to be asleep, rolled over and looked down at us through the high steel sides of his bed. "Hey, Alex," he said. "Want to hear an exploit of Fuzzle?"

Alex had heard these before; he told me once that Ted entertains the whole operating room with Fuzzle exploits, just before they put him under. He grinned and put his head back against the wall. He was wearing his green surgical cap and it was all sweaty around the forehead. He must have had emergency surgery, this late, and from the looks of his face, it hadn't gone well. Most of the time, late night surgeries at Babies are on kids from the neighborhood streets, kids with gunshot wounds, sometimes. Alex closed his eyes, to listen. "Sure," he said. "Tell me the one about Fuzzle's uncle."

Ted nodded and settled back onto his pillows, his arms bent beneath his head. He loves to tell the same exploit, over and over, expanding it each time. "One day," he began, "Fuzzle went to visit his rich old uncle."

I should have tried to stay awake to listen but I was so warm and so content that I couldn't. I drifted into sleep with Ted's voice spinning in my ears and the good solid weight of a man on my cot. I think that Alex fell asleep there for awhile too and eventually Ted slept, too. It's funny how soothing hospital sounds can be, if you're used to them: the steady counting of the machine that measured the drops of liquid nutrition into Ted's line; the beeping of his roommate's heart monitor; the almost but not quite silent humming of all the devices that keep our kids living; the quiet rubber noise of the nurses' shoes, always there, keeping watch. It's like a lullaby for these kids. Sometimes Ted can't sleep at home, without it. I often can't sleep at home, where there is only me to guard him.

Alex probably never even went home that night, because the next morning, early, he performed the princess's surgery. Even the security men couldn't keep the gypsies off the floor that morning. The campers from the park came in and the halls were packed with smoky dark people, holding vigil.

I took my morning shower and I wheeled Ted off to the 10th floor schoolroom. He always complains about the injustice of having to attend school in the hospital but I always make him go. We waited for the elevator surrounded by gypsies. It was a strange gathering, like being at a fair, the air buzzing with energy.

When I came back to 9-South I couldn't stay in Ted's room. I was restless and hungry, somehow, for the company of gypsies. So I found myself a small corner in the hall and sat down with them, and waited. Most of the women sat on couches, rolling beads through their fingers, saying a kind of rosary, I guess. The men did nothing, just leaned against the walls, their arms crossed over their chests. There were even babies and small children with them— strictly against hospital rules—crawling over the women's knees and running around the men's legs. I found myself staring at the children, strong healthy children whose faces were unmarked by pain. I wanted to hold one; I wanted to feel the body of a healthy child in my arms. I wanted to run my hands along chubby legs and to press my face into a soft, laughing, unscarred belly. I wanted to steal a gypsy child, and keep it for my own.

But I'm a polite and ordinary parent and I just sat quietly until Alex came out of the surgical wing and walked over to the gypsy parents. He was smiling. He took hold of the father's hand and shook it, as if the child had just been born. "She's just fine," he said. "She'll be fine. Perfect. No problems." A noise went up from the crowded hall, a noise I'd never heard before—the rushing sigh of collective answered prayers.

I slipped away into the parents' bathroom, the only room on the floor with a lock on the door, the only room where you get left alone, and I pressed my face against the cool tile on the wall.

That night, the gypsies celebrated. The princess was back in her room, groggy and in pain, but essentially healed. Her grandmother sat with her, while her parents laughed and danced in the lounge. Whenever I passed her room, going back and forth on my errands around the floor, the grandmother was rocking in her chair, smiling to herself, weaving together bits of colored string and straw. She was a small woman, all in black. I thought about her: she, too, must have the royal blood of the ancient race of Romany and some of their special powers.

After Ted was asleep, I went to the princess's room and stepped inside. The little girl was asleep and I stood at the foot of her high bed and looked at her. She was lovely. Her grandmother nodded at me.

"I'm glad she'll be okay," I said.

The grandmother sighed. "She will have a scar," she said. "A big scar, right across her belly. They put big ugly metal staples in her skin. Can you imagine that, stapling a baby?"

I looked down at the child's face. "It will fade," I said. "It will be just a thin white line in a few months."

She sighed again.

I tried to keep quiet, tried not to be a self-righteous, my-kid's-suffered-more-than-your-kid jerk of a parent, but

I couldn't help it. It just comes out sometimes. "My little boy has had fourteen operations," I said. "Some of his scars have been opened and re-stapled three or four times."

She looked at me, her face dark and foreign, a net of deep lines. "How can you keep from screaming?" she said. "How can you keep from cutting up these doctors, with their own knives?"

I looked at the little princess, sucking her thumb now, in her sleep. "I don't know how to scream. No one ever taught me how to scream, and now I can't learn, I guess," I said. "And then sometimes I see kids get better. Like her." I looked at the grandmother.

She made a rough sound in her throat. "Thank God, she will be better. But yours? Not yours?"

"No. Not mine." I walked toward the door and she rose and touched my arm.

"Your boy will live, though. I see it in his face. He is still curious, interested. He will live."

I felt both my hands reaching out and clasping hers. I felt the lifting of a great weight, my fortune finally told. "He will?"

She squeezed my hands. "Yes, of course he will." She smiled. "He has that cat, that fat black cat. That cat is so fat and so mean because he's swallowed so much pain." She laughed and shook her head. "What is that cat's name?"

"Fuzzle?" I said.

"Yes, yes, Fuzzle. He's a one, that Fuzzle." She dropped my hands and reached up to touch my face. "I've heard those stories he tells, your boy. Oh yes, that boy will live."

I nodded. Really, I've always known it, but it's easy to fall into doubt.

The grandmother gathered up the little triangles she'd been weaving and said, "Come on. I'm giving these to the children. For luck."

We walked along the hall and she went in and out of rooms, slipping her charms under most of the kids' pillows. I tried not to notice which children she skipped over because I knew why: only the children who are going to live will need luck, after all. But I am curious, like my son, and so I kept track. She left a charm for Richy but not for Nicole. She slipped her last charm under Ted's pillow and so there was none left for his roommate, Robby, whose mother sleeps on her cot beside her son's bed just as I do.

That whole night I lay awake listening to the songs and the laughter from the lounge. I knew that even gypsies would not light campfires inside a hospital but I imagined that they did. I imagined violin music and wild dancing around tall, leaping flames. I imagined that the fires grew, higher and higher, until they set this place ablaze. I imagined that fire, growing huge and white hot, consuming all of this and setting the children, all the children, free.

After the Women's Writing Retreat in Paradox NY: Notes for the Story I'm Afraid to Write

IN OUR WORKSHOP IN PARADOX, WE TALKED ABOUT starting stories. If you're not at all certain how a story should go, we said, begin with an exercise; fool yourself into thinking it is all play, that it doesn't really matter, that it won't hurt to try. So—

THREE STRANGE THINGS: AN EXERCISE
Here are three strange things that happened in the first twenty-four hours after I came home from Paradox. I haven't made any of them up, actually, so they are insufficiently fictionalized and in the story, of course, they will have to be symbolically related and create a nice three-part structure; I know that. [Look at notes from Glover's Writing Workshop, esp. exercises called 1) Boss Image and 2) The Third Thing. Are those notes in green notebook on baker's shelf? Check.]

THE FIRST THING
My middle sister (cushioned by her placement, relatively

unscathed) called to say that my mother said that my father attended his own funeral and, while there, spoke "intently" (my mother's word) to his old work buddy who was standing under the green canopy shading his coffin. (Naturally, I think, he wasn't talking intently to me or to my mother, wife of sixty-one years. Work—i.e. other men—still comes first.)

Sometimes, my sister reports, frequently in fact, my mother forgets that my father is dead and calls, in quite a panic (understandably), saying that she can't find him anywhere in the house or yard. Then my sister, or her husband or daughter, has to break the news all over again, something like this [See workshop notes, i.e., don't report; use dialog whenever possible.]

My sister begins. "Mom, do you remember seeing Dad in the hospital?"

My mother thinks a while, then says, "For my hysterectomy?"

My sister. "No. When Dad was sick. With cancer."

My mother snorts. "Your father has never been sick a day in his life. Never even took penicillin until he was seventy-three. I was the sick one: polio, slipped disk, gallbladder, six pregnancies." She smiles, an annoying, superior smile. "He might have complained, though. Men are such babies about pain."

Sister: "Dad was in terrible pain, Mom, and he hardly complained at all. He didn't even go to the hospital until nine days before he died. Didn't even let on he was sick until after Memorial Day weekend and by then he had ten tumors, one in almost every organ; two in some."

Mother: "I can play the organ any time I want to now. It doesn't bother him. Will you sing? Please?"

[Dialog continues. In the story, the dialog will be sharper, not so rambly, although, really, my mother does ramble. And maybe there will be room for another part here—a fourth strange thing? But all the exercises use 3 repetitions. 3 is the magical fairy tale #. But Ellen, our spiritual director at Paradox, said that 3 is only the European male magic number. That Native Peoples, instead, revere 4, the figure of balance. 4 Seasons, 4 Directions, 4 Winds, etc. So maybe I can do 4.]

So, THE (POSSIBLY) FOURTH STRANGE THING

Another of my sisters, the oldest, one of those my father molested (not raped—that was another sister, the youngest.) [There are five of us. Too many to fit comfortably into a short story and all of that terrible history is too dark for this story, anyway. Besides, incest stories are common as dirt these days, always depressing and a drag on the market.] called just before I went to Paradox, after I'd come back from the funeral, and she said that she is more afraid than ever, now that our father is dead.

My sister: "Because now I don't know where he is. Before, I knew that he was on the west coast, 3000 miles away. But now, he could be anywhere."

Me, trying to laugh. "I know where he is. I saw him in his coffin, in the red golf sweater you sent him, the one he'd never wear. I saw him; trust me, he ain't anywhere."

Her: "I'm not sure."

[Note connection: Neither is my mother, sure. But my youngest sister, bloodied at five and at fifteen and often in between, says, "When did Mother ever not decide what to remember and what to forget?" Another note: I changed "raped" to "bloodied." The word itself hurts, even though he's gone.]

Me: "Listen. For a week, I slept in his bed, in his room,

with all his stuff. Every night, I spoke into the dark, 'Okay, old man, here's your chance. I'm here. Come get me.' But he didn't. I slept fine except for the noisy swallows in the nest under the eave." [Later on, try "Things with Wings" list exercise.]

Her: "So? So maybe he wasn't there. So he could be here. He could be anywhere." Her voice takes on that little girl quality that we all recognize as a symptom of her most fragile state, her recurring vulnerability. My sister will be sixty this September, but her voice doesn't remember that, sometimes.

THE SECOND THING

How I almost shot my son Jake, the night I returned from Paradox: the hottest July 14 ever in Albany. [Look up exact temp.] It was all a farcical situation. I rode home with two other women, in their car, so there was no car in my driveway that night. When I went to bed, I left no lights on; I slept in the spare room (cooler), with noisy fans blowing, hearing nothing, until.... [Stretch out this moment; build suspense.] Jake came in, quietly, using his key, having drunk too many beers to drive, being wise, just like I always tell him. He fell asleep on the couch downstairs. Around 4:30 a.m. he got up to pee, in the downstairs bathroom, and then I did hear something. I got up, terrified that it was a bat, [We get bats every summer. Put bats in "Things with Wings" list.] and crept to the head of the stairs. I turned on the hall light, so that the bat wouldn't fly upstairs. The light woke, and terrified, Jake, who had thought the house was empty. I heard something—his intake of startled breath maybe, and knew that this was no bat. I had just put my trembling hand on the phone to call 911, blood pounding in my chest and ears, when Jake began to walk up the stairs, intending to foil the intruder he imagined. I stood paralyzed at the top, hearing those carefully quiet footsteps ascending. And there we met. [This is a perfect dramatic moment. But a little silly, maybe, sitcom Lucy and Ricky stuff. And, technically, it will be tricky, requiring a sudden switch in "camera angle" so that the story's "I," the narrator, can see her own face. See Burroway, *Writing Fiction*, on pt. of view.] I can just picture our faces—one looking up, one down, but both wearing identical masks of fear that turn to simultaneous relief as we recognize each other. Then I can hear our hysterical, knee-buckling laughter. [Try to use all the senses. Smell and taste are difficult here. What do "fear" and "relief" taste like?]

[That first line, the almost-shooting part, is imaginary or at least after-the-event, so maybe I am beginning to fictionalize here. I only thought about it later, in the tingling horror of realizing I *might* have, if I'd had a gun. A terrible warning: It is possible to hurt your own child. But maybe it adds drama, something this story needs. See Burroway: "Only trouble is interesting."]

[Possible connection: my oldest sister's fears—if we don't know who is there, in our darkened rooms at night, it could always be my father, couldn't it? My father—time/space traveler now, set free in the dark?]

[Look for that card, the one with the light blue cover that says "With sympathy in the loss of your father." That "in" really bothers me. Is it just the wrong preposition, as I hope, or is it a sign? Are we all caught, now, "in" this death, together?]

THE THIRD THING
On July 15, at 6:30 a.m., after I've finally gotten back to sleep in my own room—Jake now in the spare room—the largest storm in twenty years hits Albany. I hear it roar in like a train [cliché, but that's the only thing it sounded like]

just as sirens go off all over the city: a too-late warning.
[Use quotes from paper—*Albany Times-Union*, July 16—
for authenticity. E.g., "5 Dead as Rampaging Storm Inter-
rupts Heat Wave" (A1). "At 6:41 a.m., the National
Weather Service at Albany County Airport clocked winds
at 77 mph" (A1). "This type of storm system, which is self-
perpetuating, is also known as a derecho, which describes
its rapid movement and destructive winds" (A2). "The sau-
cer-shaped mesoscale convective complex is a nocturnal
beast, building its energy through the night before awak-
ening at sunrise" (A2).]

Nothing much happens to my yard in the storm, just a
maple branch flung fifty feet, coming to rest against the
back door. That's the worst of it and I can move that alone.
(Later, someone warns me not to sit under the maple tree
for a while: its branches may have been weakened and they
can fall at any time, without warning, even when there is
no wind.) Two blocks away, though, whole trees and power
poles fell and the road is closed all day, while chain saws
whine. [Note caption for photo in *T-U*: "A traffic light is
still working after it was downed by the storm along West-
ern Avenue near North Main in Albany" (A3).] Jake slept
right through the whole thing, his head full of the noise of
the fan. [But surely a storm this unusual, this fierce, must
be symbolic of great discord, right? See Nabokov's story
"Signs and Symbols" in Burroway. Hell, see *King Lear*.]

Later that morning, I decide to rinse off my tiny clay
Mother Goddess and Crone figures—they look dusty and
unloved—and I decide to give the Crone (I always try to
soothe the Crone) a sprig of fresh lavender from the garden, to hold in the thumb-shaped depression the potter
has left in her skirts. The lavender is in honor of Ellen's
storytelling workshop at Paradox and her poem "The Shawl
Dance" which features a particularly scary crone. And the

lavender and sage she burnt as incense to consecrate our reading space, the old boathouse, our first night in Paradox. I run cool water from the faucet over the figures and, too late, realize that the tiny round baby (a small clay pebble, really, with carved baby features and a round o mouth) which fits into the Mother Goddess's indented belly will be washed right out of its womb-spot and although I try, with a frantic futile grab, to stop it, be carried down the drain with the force of the water. [Fix that sentence.] I turn off the faucet and stare into the dark, empty hole of the drain. I'm not sure if I should be frightened or if I should laugh—I have lost the baby, after all; I have let the baby disappear into the wet swirling darkness [think of that symbolism!]. But perhaps I can adopt the healthy spiritual attitude Ellen has spent all week inculcating into all of our tremulous souls and see this washing-away as a sign of cleansing, of change, of magical transformation, see that clay-pebble baby set free in the watery universe of the sewers which flow away from Albany, today so flush and rushing with the waters from the storm. [Note: look up— where does Albany drain water go, really? The river?] I opt for the positive. Do I have a choice, really? Should I sit quivering in my kitchen, awaiting retribution? I give all of the lavender to the Mother Goddess, packing it gently into her bereft belly. [In the story, maybe the MG, like me, can learn to welcome menopause?] I remember the tiny pinecone I brought back from Paradox and that I place, reverently enough I hope, in the Crone's expectant lap. I think I've satisfied the spirits but you can never be sure. Even thinking I have is probably a bad sign, in itself, just the kind of dangerous self-congratulation that the spirits love to answer with sudden, crushing humiliation.

[The story is not going well. There is no plot emerging here. It's all intersections and no roads. A too-too tangled web. So here's another exercise to spur the story on. This is Glover's "List Thing."]

LIST #1: THINGS WITH WINGS
The birds at Paradox: hummers, herons, and loons, weaving across the blue sky every morning, partner and counterpoint to the clear blue lake below.

Dragonflies: The afternoon I spent my free time on a lakeside rock and hundreds of dragonflies spun above the water, a dragonfly ballet. One pair, joined at the abdomen [Look up: how and where, anatomically, do dragonflies mate?] rest on my knee for some time.

Bees: The day I returned home, that hottest July 14 ever, I found bees swarming all over the slimy green water in the birdbath. Without a second's thought (although I am allergic to bee stings), I waded into the swarm, dumped the water out, and brought the hose to refill the birdbath with fresh, sparkling water. [Like the lake?] As I turned the hose on, I realized my mistake—a huge cloud of bees descended in buzzing thirst, to charge the hose and the arms which held it. I prayed that my good intentions would save me. [See fairy tale handout, storytelling workshop. Blue folder.] I prayed for the bees to recognize the redemptive kindness in my gesture. I stood very still, keeping the hose straight, and refilled the birdbath, all from within that welter of bees. I was not stung. (I'm not sure how many stings it would take to kill me. Not many, I've been told.) The bees flung themselves into the clean water [baptism image?] with fierce abandon. I watched them; they had totally forgotten me. Each bee floated on the surface of the water and then rose into the air, heavy with absorbed water, and flew, painfully, carrying its burden of moisture back to the mother hive.

But many didn't make it. Weighted by water, they fell from the sky and lay, worn out and barely struggling, on the hot ground. See? Their good, selfless intentions didn't save them. [Note: maybe this is really another "strange thing." Can I have five? Should the bee thing replace #2? But I need the bat from #2, to foreshadow the other bat. See below. This whole thing is getting messy.]

Butterflies: My oldest sister believes in good ghosts, too. She sees her son Bobby's spirit in butterflies and she finds some comfort in their company. [But I haven't really seen any butterflies, home or in Paradox. I think I just put them in so I wouldn't feel so sad about the bees. But they'll have to go. See Burroway on consistent tone.]

Bats: One night at Paradox, a bat flew into the boathouse just as we had finished our readings and were congratulating one another on our collective strength and beauty and courage. The bat swooped over the heads of 24 cowering women and Ellen tried to calm us by telling us that the bat is a benign symbol of transformation—a wonderful creature who always appears in the enchanted limbo between darkness and light. I tried hard to believe her and maybe it worked, for a while, because there, surrounded by women, I did not scream and crouch down with my arms around my head. But at home, when summer bats fling themselves through the darkling upstairs hall, I cannot be calm. (Remember when I thought Jake was a bat, and I in my house alone?) Perhaps I am not ready for all this transformation.

LIST #2: THINGS WITHOUT WINGS
Duffy, summer rent-a-cat at Paradox, to be returned to the pound in September

Snake on path, fat and gorged with mouse
Grandmother Spider
Blue-gills, fish in lake
Elephants [A long story, will never fit. Never mind.]
That lavender and sage, burnt as offering. [But, as smoke,
it almost has wings. Switch lists?]

[This list is very sketchy because as I was writing it (really,
I couldn't make anything like this up and besides, the phone
call will reappear, transformed into numbers, on the AT&T
records), my old friend Lorry called, after two years. That
last time, two years ago, her voice had been shaky—she'd
just had a small black melanoma removed from her arm
and she was thinking about dying at forty. Today, she told
me that she had had a baby, a little girl, at forty-two. All
was well. Lorry named her baby Eliza. [Get this: one of
my sisters is named *Elizabeth*; she is another of the badly
wounded ones. She has recently called to tell me that she
has been having terrible flashbacks since our father died
and even more terrible dreams. Dreams in which she is the
abuser and her victim is the little girl named Lizzie, the
little girl with thick red braids. (Look up incest survivors
and dreams.) Lorry's little Eliza was born on June 9, she
says. My father died on June 10.]
    [I'm stopping for today. This story is going all wrong.
The exercises aren't working. There is too much in it. It
will be much too long and I really wanted a short-short—
simple, clean and better for the market. I wanted it to stay
under 5 pages.
    But I'm afraid I know how it will have to end. I've be-
gun to hear the last lines sounding in my head, something
like this:

    The storm and the strangeness; the water and the bees;
the bat—all these are proof. My father really has gotten

loose in the universe; he has grown huge in death, become a mesoscalic complex, a nocturnal beast. My father has become a derecho. Mother Goddess, forgive me—I didn't mean to drown your baby. Mother Goddess, protect little Eliza, little Lizzie. Mother Goddess, help us all.]

Is that all right? Is that enough to placate the gods? I have always believed in imagining the worst, the very worst. If you do, it will not happen. You are in control.

So no, this time it will end differently. My father will rest quiet in his red-sweater grave. He will stay put, just as I last saw him—a frail old man, brave at the end, and almost worthy of our sorrow. I will tell the story differently this time, I promise. Ellen said, promise yourself a reward, something nice to help you through the bad times. Remember, the good are always rewarded in fairy tales. [But not bees.] Here is my reward: I will give myself a gift, if I can end this story right. I will take this story to Paradox, next summer, and I will read it aloud to the circle of women in our consecrated boathouse. I can see it: when I am done reading, the women rise and close the circle, wrapping their soft full arms around me. The bat weaves above our heads like a blessing and I am not afraid.

One more thing: Next year, I will bring my sisters to Paradox. Surely there is room for 4 more. We will not disturb the balance.

A Note on the Author

Hollis Seamon's stories have appeared in many publications, including *Chicago Review*, *The Hudson Review*, *CALYX*, *The American Voice*, and *13th Moon*. She teaches writing and literature at The College of Saint Rose in Albany, New York.

A Note on the Cover Artist

Deborah Zlotsky has exhibited her paintings nationally. The title of the entire work, from which individual painting were selected for the cover, is *Body Parts*. She teaches painting and drawing at the College of Saint Rose in Albany, New York.

A Note on the Type

The type used in this book is Adobe Jenson, a contemporary version of the typeface produced by Nicolas Jenson in Venice in 1470 when printing first began. Jenson's type has never gone out of fashion. The digitized type used here, drawn by Robert Slimbach, is faithful to the original.